Mountain Biking In Northern New Mexico

Historical and Natural History Rides

Craig Martin

Mountain Biking In Northern New Mexico

Historical and Natural History Rides

University of New Mexico Press
Albuquerque

Library of Congress
Cataloging-in-Publication Data
— — — — — — — — — — — — — — —
Martin, Craig, 1952–
Mountain biking in northern New Mexico
Craig Martin.
    p.   c.m.—(Coyote series)
Includes index.
ISBN 0-8263-1511-9
1. All terrain cycling—New Mexico—Guidebooks.
2. New Mexico—Guidebooks. I. Title. II. Series.
GV1045.5.N6M37 1994
796.6'4'09789—dc20
93-49530
CIP

For my sister, Barb, whose
spirit and courage inspire
all whose lives she touches

Contents

PART 4
Volcanoes, Mines,
Rocks, and Minerals

Cautionary Note ...

By nature, mountain bike riding is a hazardous activity, and all riders must assume the risk associated with the sport. Although the author has tried to warn the reader of any hazards that may be encountered along the trails, conditions change with weather, season, and trail use. Also, riders come to trails with varying abilities. They should keep in mind their own skills and fitness level before attempting any of the rides. This book offers only guidelines: the final responsibility is in the hands of the rider. Riders should know their limitations, prepare properly, and use good judgment. The author can assume no responsibility for any injuries or hardships resulting from any ride featured herein.

Preface

Hal Coss, chief ranger and my boss at Saguaro National Monument, walked into work one Monday morning with his left arm tightly tied to his chest by a sling. Known for his love of the natural world and ability to outrun those of us who were twenty years his junior, Hal was always trying new ways to have fun outdoors. "What have you done now?" I teased. "I went over the handle bars of my *mountain bike*," Hal replied. It was the first time I had ever heard the words *mountain* and *bike* together. Listening to Hal enthusiastically describe the events leading up to his accident, I vowed that whatever a mountain bike was I would protect the unity of my bones and never get near one. Hal mended quickly and was soon back on his bike; foolishly, I kept that promise to myself, stayed away from mountain bikes, and missed out on eight years of fun.

Discovering that hordes of normal folks were pedaling bikes with fat tires, I finally cast aside my pride and fell in love with traveling the back roads and trails on two wheels. I wasn't long into my biking career before I noticed that too often the scenery at trailside was ignored as I concentrated exclusively on the rocky path, pedaling furiously to master twenty-mile loops. Although I was having a good time and keeping fit, I wanted something more from a ride.

Preface

The trips I enjoyed most led somewhere: the ride was important, but so were the terrain it covered and the destination. I searched for mountain bike *tours*, not mere loops to ride around. I used my mountain bike to take me to ghost towns, along abandoned railroad grades, to fossil locations, and natural arches, and amid extensive volcanic fields. It was possible to have a challenging ride and pedal to fun places!

Often after a ride, I headed to the library to learn more about places and things on the trail. My naturalist training got me thinking about how exciting it would be to lead interpretive mountain bike tours. However, this would be an impractical format, and putting the rides in book form has satisfied my desire to share them with others.

Collected in these pages are the best mountain bike *explorations* available to riders in northern New Mexico. I hope to draw hard-core riders—those who shoot past me as I struggle through those twenty-mile loops—into trying something new, slowing down, and paying more attention to what is along the route than to the route itself. For the casual riders—those who can't, or choose not to, train for extremes of physical exertion—these explorations offer a way to enjoy touring the backcountry by bicycle without feeling that they have to keep up with every spandex-clad rider who blows by.

As I was finishing *Fly-Fishing in Northern New Mexico,* I discussed with Jeff Grathwohl, mountain bike enthusiast and former editor at The University of New Mexico Press, the possibility of a mountain bike guidebook, but with no time to work on it the project was shelved. A year later, Jeff left New Mexico, but I was fortunate that another mountain-biking editor took his place, Andrea Otañez. She persuaded me to revive the project. Without Jeff and Andrea's encouragement and support, this book would have died a quiet death, entombed as magnetic bits deep within forgotten corners of my computer's hard disk.

On the trail, in the office, and over the phone, a small horde of friendly folks took the time to offer information on trails, route conditions, and land ownership. Particularly helpful and deserving of thanks are staff members at the Bureau of Land Management. Erica McLean, recreation technician at the Rio Puerco Resource Area, carefully mapped out the Cabezon area to steer me clear of private land and the Cabezon Wilderness Study Area. Chuck Schultz and M. J. Chavez of the Taos Resource Area provided details about the Chili Line through Comanche Canyon, helped me avoid potential problems with landowners, and ignited my enthusiasm about the possibility of establishing parts of the Chili Line as a multi-use trail. At El Malpais, Ranger Rick Jones, long ago a co-worker at Saguaro National Monument, led me to the wonderful Brazo Area and opened up a whole new part of the world to explore by bike.

As a scientist in the unfamiliar territory of historical research, I welcomed the assistance of patient librarians and historians, who never quite made the connection between mountain bikes and history. Dinah Jentgen of the New Mexico Highway Department generously offered her files on the road up La Bajada Hill. Theresa Strottman scouted the archives at the Los Alamos Historical Society Archives and found sources that allowed me to piece together the background on the Garcia Homestead. Gabrielle Palmer, director of the Camino Real Project, took the time to answer a multitude of questions on the route of the Camino Real and the early history of La Bajada Hill. The competence of Arthur Olivas of the Museum of New Mexico and Paul Savedra at the New Mexico State Archives made assembling historical photographs a breeze.

A few others deserve mention and heartfelt thanks. Mark Gruber field tested ride descriptions, and offered suggestions on improving route directions. Cartographer Andrea Kron graciously offered suggestions on how to make the maps better and introduced me to drawing maps by computer, saving many hours of tedious work. Susan Newcomb, a recent transplant from New Jersey who at first had no idea what a mountain bike was, provided worry-free child care while I was in the saddle doing field research. As always, June Fabryka-Martin, my wife, helped with editing the first draft, proofreading, criticizing maps and ride profiles, sharing rides, and offering her unhesitating support of my time-consuming hobbies. Without her understanding and encouragement, this book would never have been written. Two little people who made the biggest contribution to this project are my children, Jessica and Alex, for without them to care for, I would have to work outside the home with no opportunity to spend my free time writing.

My great personal paradox is this: I spend much of my time in the outdoors—on foot, skis, mountain bike, or with flyrod in hand—searching for quiet places away from the crowd, and then, for some unexplainable reason, enjoy sharing those discoveries with others. My justification is the hope that others who discover and come to love New Mexico's hidden treasures will be inspired to help in the fight to preserve the state's historical, cultural, and natural resources. I urge readers to seek out and support both national and local organizations whose goals are to preserve history and environment. Letters to state and national government officials are another effective weapon against the destruction of our heritage: one person who expresses a written opinion to a legislator is worth five hundred who remain silent. To continue my support of conservation efforts in the state, I pledge to donate 20 percent of the royalties from this book to organizations active in maintaining New Mexico's resources.

I confess it was a joy researching the twenty-five rides on the following pages. Particularly memorable are the first looks at Hagan and La Liendre, the solitude of the Cabezon and Cebolla Canyon areas, the striking views from Chino Mesa and Picuris Peak, finding wagon ruts on La Bajada Hill, and the challenge of discovering each yard of the Chili Line at Barranca Hill. May the readers and riders who use this book come away with the same excitement I felt on each of these tours and experience a closer link with New Mexico's rich history and dramatic geology.

Introduction:
Touring the Land of
Enchantment

New Mexico's intriguing history is the story of three peoples and their evolving cultures. For each, change came both from within and from sharing the land with the others. From Anasazi to Pueblo, Spanish to Mexican, and Anglo culture imported from the "States" and regionalized to meet the unusual character of its new home, New Mexico's people have always learned to adapt. As each group struggled against and learned to live with the others, it left behind distinct reminders of its way of life. This rich cultural tapestry lies waiting to be explored in the form of Anasazi ruins, the remains of Spanish farming communities, the ghosts of mining towns, abandoned railroad grades, and historic roads, all ready to tell their tales to the patient traveller willing to take the time to listen and observe.

Threaded with the tapestry of human history is the fabric of the landscape. New Mexico is a land of contrasts: high mountains and rubble-filled valleys, stately conifer forests and open desert grasslands, isolated volcanoes and former ocean floors, demanding farmland and hard-rock mines. Like the artifacts of human history, the land itself has stories to tell. Some tales are of changes eons in the making, such as the one of an ancient floodplain uplifted to become an unending desert of shifting sand dunes; others

1

are born of fire and red flowing lava; and others tell of incomprehensible heat and pressure that takes ordinary rock and transforms it into stones of exquisite shape and color. The most surprising tales are the most recent. They tell of the people who settled New Mexico and dramatically reshaped in only a few hundred years parts of the landscape that had taken millions of years to develop.

Exploring New Mexico's history and geology has long been a rewarding pastime for residents and visitors. The growing popularity of the mountain bike has created a new way to delve into history. Riding a mountain bike into New Mexico's past doubles the pleasure of exploration. The enjoyment of riding is amplified when following a route to an exciting destination. Mountain biking also opens up places too difficult to reach by other means. As an alternative vehicle, a mountain bike can be used as a poor man's four-wheel drive to reach destinations too far to walk, too rough to drive. This book strives to offer the reader the best of two worlds: a good ride leading to an interesting place.

Preparing for the Terrain and Weather

Before setting out on the trail, mountain bike riders need to consider ways to ensure their trip will be safe as well as pleasant. Under the blazing blue sky of the Land of Enchantment, weather may seem the least of the worries facing a rider, but ideal weather conditions are the exception in New Mexico. Wind, precipitation, and extremes in temperature can all cause unexpected and potentially dangerous situations. By planning properly, riders should enter the backcountry prepared for most hazardous weather conditions.

Throughout northern New Mexico, winter snows make mountain riding difficult or impossible. Winter rides are confined to lower elevations and clear spells that dry out the roads. Spring comes late, if at all, with days that begin with winter's cold temperatures yet heat up rapidly under the springtime sun. During a long spring day, riders can expect to experience every season's temperatures. Spring rides require a full range of clothing, from warm jackets for morning or late afternoon to warm-weather gear such as shorts and loose bicycle shirts for midday. To adjust to changing temperatures, riders should dress in layers that can easily be shed or added.

2

Introduction

Spring is New Mexico's windiest season. As a continuous string of cold fronts move in from the west, riders should be prepared to face stiff breezes and blowing dust. The most enjoyable spring trips are ridden on the rare calm days between fronts. A potentially serious circumstance in spring is a sudden change from mild to cold weather. With the arrival of a cold front, temperatures can drop twenty-five degrees Fahrenheit in a half-hour, and cold rain or even snow can descend on the mountains. When setting off on a spring ride, riders should have a recent weather forecast in hand and always carry clothing appropriate to meet sudden and extreme changes in weather.

The New Mexican summer is really two separate seasons. Late May through mid-July is characterized by cloudless days and high daily temperatures that may exceed one hundred degrees Fahrenheit at lower elevations. Mountain bike trips under these conditions require early starts, intelligent pacing, plenty of water, and copious sunblock. Riders in the mountains will experience the full range of temperatures, from near freezing early in the morning to as high as eighty-five degrees Fahrenheit by afternoon. For comfort, start with a warm jacket and shed down to shorts as the day progresses. Applying frequent and plentiful coats of sunblock will reduce the risk of sunburn.

Mid-July through early September marks the rainy season in northern New Mexico. Clear mornings quickly give way to cloudy skies as rising hot air creates a thunderhead over each peak. By noon, thunderstorms are rumbling in the mountains. These storms are accompanied by heavy rain, high winds, and violent lightning. To avoid the storms, mid-summer bike rides are best completed by noon. Still, riders should always assume they will get wet during a summer ride. Carrying rain gear is essential as is allowing extra time for delays and more difficult riding conditions on muddy roads.

Fall is the favorite season of many New Mexicans as warm, sunny days and cool, cloudless nights prevail. Windy or rainy days are infrequent, making mountain bike route conditions ideal. Riding is enjoyable up to the first snows of winter, which usually occur in early November but are possible in mid-October. Riders should know the weather forecast before heading out on a fall trip: riding through an unexpected snowstorm in shorts and a T-shirt can easily lead to hypothermia.

The riding seasons suggested in Table 1 are based on an average year—which rarely occurs. In general, explore the trails below 7,500 feet in winter, spring or fall, as snow conditions allow; these trails are often too hot for comfortable summer riding. Trails above 7,500 feet usually open by mid-May, but after a dry winter may be rideable by mid-April. Avoid dirt roads after periods of heavy thunderstorms, or immediately after winter or spring snows.

Table 1. Best Season for Each Ride

Winter

Hagan, Coyote, and Tonque	Where's Waldo?
Cabezon	La Bajada Hill
Otowi to Buckman	Window Rock

Spring and Fall

La Liendre	Garcia Homestead
Amoxiumqua	Barranca Hill
Chino Mesa	Twenty-nine Volcano Loop
El Malpais	Rim Vista

Summer

Midnight, Anchor, and La Belle	Red River Pass and the Big Ditch
Pioneer Canyon	Cebolla Canyon
Picuris Peak	Santa Fe Trail Ruts
Old Bland Road	Santa Fe Northwestern Railway
Jarita Mesa Mines	Fairy Crosses in Arroyo Hondo
Teakettle Rock	

No matter what the season, riding at high elevations in the mountains brings a few special problems to visitors and natives alike. Riders should be prepared for extra exertion due to less oxygen at higher altitudes. Those unaccustomed to biking in thin air should allow some time to acclimate to the mountains by first attempting rides at lower elevations, then working up to rides in the highest country. Even after an adjustment period, visitors should take it easy on the higher routes. Exhaustion is not the only potential hazard. Riders should be aware of mountain sickness, an illness caused by rapid ascent to high elevation and characterized by headache, nausea, weakness and general discomfort. Riders experiencing these symptoms should descend to a lower elevation; if symptoms persist, medical attention may be required.

High altitude also means increased exposure to the ultraviolet radiation from the sun. With less atmosphere to shield the skin, riders must provide their own protection in the form of sunblock. Apply sunblock to all exposed skin—hands, face, arms, and legs—and while touring, reapply at least every three hours. Also essential are sunglasses that block at least 95 percent of ultra-violet light.

Equipment

Coming prepared for a ride in the backcountry can be a matter not only of safety but survival. Mountain conditions can take the uninitiated by surprise, with disastrous results. Riders should pack simply but be prepared for the worst.

The most important piece of equipment is a helmet. Although uncomfortable and awkward, head protection is essential under all trail conditions, particularly on steep and rocky roads where it is easy to lose control. Riding gloves are another important safety item. By providing a solid grip and preventing hand fatigue, they allow for greater control, especially when riders are tired at the end of a long day. Gloves also protect the hands during falls. Stiff-soled shoes will prevent fatigue and provide solid traction when pushing a bike on a steep climb.

Water is important to any mountain bike rider in the arid mountains of New Mexico. Without a constant supply of fluid, a rider will quickly become dehydrated by dry air, intense sunlight, and physical exertion. Water bottles should be carried on the bike frame, as well as an extra supply in a backpack; a half-gallon of water per ride is a minimum. There should also be an emergency supply of water in the support vehicle. With potentially harmful giardia bacteria found in all watersheds, it is unwise to drink untreated water from streams.

When riding a mountain bike into the backcountry, expect the unexpected, and carry a tool kit. Even when in good repair, the punishment taken by the bicycle on rocky dirt roads quickly leads to major or minor breakdowns, usually at the point where the route is farthest from civilization. Riders should be prepared to fix a flat tire, tighten any nut or screw on their bicycle (including the crank), lubricate the chain and freewheel after repeated stream crossings or long miles in the dust, and adjust brakes and derailleurs. Table 2 lists the items recommended for a basic repair kit. It is advisable to learn the skills required to repair a bicycle at home, not in an emergency fifteen miles from the nearest help.

Table 2. A Simple Mountain Bike Repair Kit

tire irons	flat-head screwdriver
tube repair kit	Phillips-head screwdriver
pliers	small adjustable wrench
Allen wrenches	chain tool
chain lubricant	crank tool
tire pump	pocket knife

Practice by performing routine bicycle maintenance before and after each trip.

Maps are important to carry on any mountain bike ride. The sketch maps in this book show routes and landmarks for navigation but admittedly will not help much if the rider is disoriented or lost. For the sake of clarity, many side roads and features of the landscape are omitted. Small secondary roads and faint tracks can lead the rider off an intended route, and it is difficult to anticipate all the possible mistakes a rider can make. Most rides are easy to follow, and the sketch maps herein will suffice. However, some rides traverse terrain laced with side roads, are in remote locations, or are potentially confusing. Carrying the USGS topographic quadrangles is recommended for the following rides: Cabezon, Red River Pass and the Big Ditch, Chino Mesa, Twenty-nine Volcano Loop, Rim Vista, Teakettle Rock and Jarita Mesa. Make certain you know how to read a topographic map before setting out on any of these trips.

Respecting the Environment

As relatively new users of public lands, mountain bike riders are often met with suspicion, and mountain bikes have acquired an undeserved reputation as being damaging of the landscape. However, a careful mountain bike rider will have no more impact on the land than other trail users and probably much less

MAP LEGEND

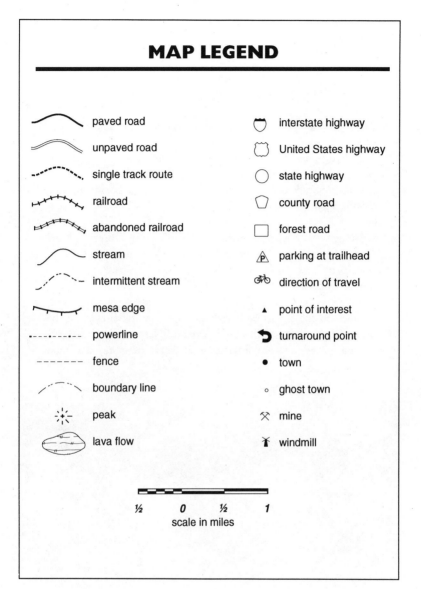

paved road		interstate highway	
unpaved road		United States highway	
single track route		state highway	
railroad		county road	
abandoned railroad		forest road	
stream		parking at trailhead	
intermittent stream		direction of travel	
mesa edge		point of interest	
powerline		turnaround point	
fence		town	
boundary line		ghost town	
peak		mine	
lava flow		windmill	

½   0   ½   1
scale in miles

than horseback riders. Whatever the truth may be, it is the perception that counts. With that in mind, riders need to be overly cautious in their use of public trails.

Like all outdoor recreationists, riders should treat public lands as the valuable and fragile resource they are. Minimizing impacts on the land should be a concern of every rider. Each rider should also remember that all mountain bikers will be judged by his or her actions. Riders should observe the following guidelines, based on the suggestions of the National Off-road Bicycle Association.

1. To minimize impacts to the environment, always stay on the trail. In arid climates, fragile soils take many years to develop and are easily damaged; tracks made in open country can remain for years.

2. To prevent trail damage, do not short cut switchbacks, and avoid riding in muddy conditions.

3. Be courteous to other trail users and maintain control of your bicycle at all times. Always yield to non-mechanized users. Horses are easily spooked by bikes: if you encounter a horse, carefully dismount, push your bike off the trail, and allow the horse to pass.

4. Respect the land and other users of the land. Observe all private property signs. Leave gates as you find them, and do not disturb livestock or wildlife. Respect trail closures and do not ride in wilderness areas. Pack out all of your trash.

5. To ensure mountain bikes' future access to sensitive areas, keep bicycles on the roads, and walk through historic sites along the trail. Help preserve the fragile remains of New Mexico history by staying off the ruins and leaving all artifacts where they are found.

Rough Trails, Like the Road Down La Bajada Hill, Require Careful Attention.

How to Use This Book
• • • • • • • • • • • • • • • • • • • •

The rides described in this book are not the usual mountain-biking fare. Readers will find few neatly closed loops or long circuits without disrupting side trips. The rides are not shaped as much by the terrain as by what is found along the way. Some tour distances are long; the routes are not merely rides, but true explorations. Rather than being opportunities to go all out and attack the hills and pedal a loop as fast as possible, the rides are intended as all-day excursions into the backcountry. Riders should take it easy and enjoy a leisurely pace, making frequent stops to poke around and find not only the features pointed out in the text, but also the many additional treasures that await careful observers. To add to an appreciation of the destination, many rides suggest short hikes away from the route.

Twenty-five mountain bike explorations are presented here, each focussing on part of New Mexico's historical or geological past. To make the rider's enjoyment of each destination more com-

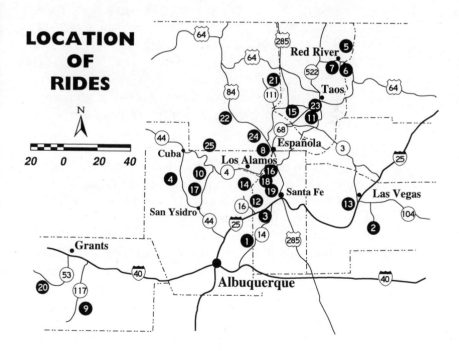

LOCATION
OF
RIDES

N

20 0 20 40

plete, background information is provided. In order to familiarize yourself with terms and to know what to look for on the trail, read the background section before taking the ride. Think of it as riding along with a naturalist whose job it is to help you understand the landscape—without too much intrusion into the ride. For those whose imagination is stimulated by a ride, suggested further reading is given.

This book was originally envisioned as a series of ride possibilities for families to enjoy together. Although the difficult nature of mountain biking in New Mexico dictated a broader focus, several routes—notably Otowi to Buckman; Where's Waldo; La Liendre; the Santa Fe Northwestern Railway; Jarita Mesa Mines; and Midnight, Anchor, and La Belle—are suitable for day-long family excursions. These rides offer not only biking opportunities, but also a chance to collect minerals, pan for gold, fish for trout, or explore a ghost town.

At high altitude, there is no such thing as an easy mountain bike ride. Most of the rides that follow require a moderate degree of fitness to complete, but riders need not be single-minded pedaling machines to complete these tours. Even casual riders will find most of them enjoyable, provided they keep in mind that the goal is to explore and have fun. There is nothing shameful about pushing a bike up or down the steeper hills.

Every mountain bike rider has his own level of skill and endurance, making it hard for one rider to judge the problems others will experience on a trail. To help prevent any surprises about difficulty, each ride description includes a summary and an elevation profile. Skill level designations are meant only as a general guide, incorporating evaluations of length, required fitness and endurance, and road surface. The classifications are slanted on the side of beginning and intermediate riders; hard-core riders will find few, if any, truly difficult rides in this book. A ride is classified as "easy" if beginners can pedal the entire loop without pushing their bikes uphill or over rough riding surfaces. "Difficult" rides are long, have a rough riding surface, or include plenty of steep uphill climbs. Anything between these extremes is called "moderate," but riders should be aware that routes in this group can have difficult stretches.

Riders questioning their ability to tackle a specific ride should look carefully at three items: distance, elevation change, and elevation profile. Elevation change is the total amount of climbing that must be done on the ride—and hence the total amount of descent. Long rides with less than one thousand feet of elevation

Table 3. Relative Difficulty of the Rides

Name	Skill level	Distance in miles	Elevation change in feet
SFNW Railway	Easy	10	400
Otowi to Buckman	Easy	8	200
Midnight, Anchor and La Belle	Easy	6	500
Santa Fe Trail Ruts	Easy	14	700
El Malpais	Easy	16	500
Where's Waldo	Easy	13	900
La Liendre	Easy	23	400
Hagan, Coyote and Tonque	Easy	24	900
Jarita Mesa	Moderate	15	1100
Window Rock	Moderate	11	800
La Bajada	Moderate	12	900
Red River Pass / Big Ditch	Moderate	10	1100
Arroyo Hondo	Moderate	10	1500
Amoxiumqua	Moderate	22	1200
Chino Mesa	Moderate	23	1200
Old Bland Road	Moderate	18	2000
Garcia Homestead	Moderate	24	1900
Cabezon	Moderate	26	1200
Pioneer Canyon	Difficult	8	1600
Rim Vista	Difficult	31	1000
Twenty-nine Volcano Loop	Difficult	27	1800
Teakettle Rock	Difficult	30	3000
Picuris Peak	Difficult	17	3200
Barranca Hill	Difficult	25	1100

change can be ridden by any reasonably fit individual. Rides with over one thousand feet of elevation change will be difficult for riders unaccustomed to high elevation. Even a ride with a small range of elevation can include several climbs and descents that make it more difficult than it appears. Use the ride profile to judge how many climbs and descents are found along the route. Table 3 lists the rides by difficulty, loosely arranged from easiest to most difficult. To get a feel for the ratings, start with an easy ride before trying the moderate and advanced ones.

Riding ability and fitness are not the only skills required for the explorations found in this book. Searching the historic or geologic past requires careful observation and much imagination. To get a true sense of the past, riders need to picture what conditions were like one hundred or one hundred million years ago. Surveying the present landscape and filling an empty street with a bustling throng on its way to work in the mines, or feeling the strain on a team of horses hauling a wagon load of freight up an impossibly steep slope, or removing a five-thousand-foot volcano from the landscape requires parking a bicycle and turning the eye inward. Find excitement in the little things: petroglyphs, railroad spikes, pot shards, rotting timbers, or volcanic bombs. These tangible relics from the past can be the link to a deeper sense of history. Ride slowly, and allow plenty of time to experience the enchanting cultural mix of New Mexico.

PART 1

Ghosts from the Past

Chapter 1
Hagan, Coyote, and Tonque Pueblo

■■■■■■■■■■■■■■■■■■■■■■■■■■■■■■■

Location: southwest of Santa Fe, northeast of
    Albuquerque

Distance: 24 miles

Elevation: 5,500 to 6,300 feet

Elevation Change: 900 feet

Skill Level: easy

Seasons: dry periods from mid-March to May,
    September to December

Ride Surface: gravel and dirt roads

Interesting Features: pueblo ruins, ghost towns, old
    railroad grade, fossils, interesting geology

Map: USGS Hagan 7.5-minute quadrangle

Access

● ● ● ● ● ● ● ● ● ● ● ● ● ● ● ● ● ●

From Santa Fe, take NM 14 south from the I-25 inter-
change. Travel about thirty-three miles through Cerrillos, Madrid
and Golden. About three miles south of Golden, turn at the intersection with Puertecito Road, a dirt road coming in from the right
(west). From Albuquerque, go east on I-40 to the Tijeras/Cedar
Crest exit, then go north on NM 14. Travel about fifteen miles,
through Cedar Crest, past the road to Sandia Crest, and to the
Santa Fe County line. Past the line, turn onto Puertecito Road.
Puertecito Road passes through private land but is open to public
travel. If the road is dry and unrutted, drive 3.5 miles and park on
the roadside just before the road makes a steep descent into a deep
arroyo.

HAGAN, COYOTE, AND TONQUE PUEBLO

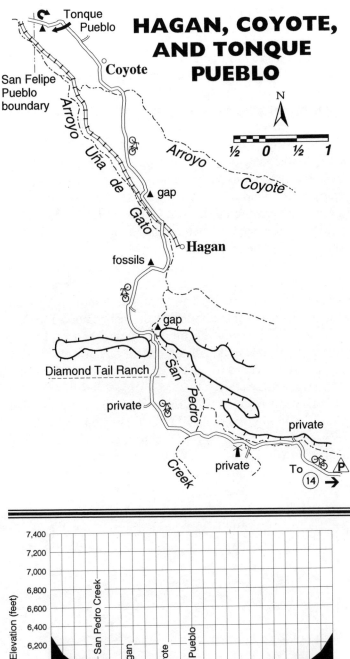

Tonque Pueblo

Coyote

San Felipe Pueblo boundary

Arroyo Uña de Gato

N

½ 0 ½ 1

Arroyo Coyote

▲ gap

Hagan

fossils ▲

gap

Diamond Tail Ranch

San Pedro

private

private

private

To (14) →

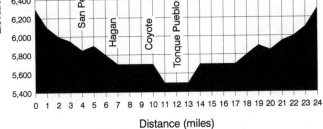

Elevation (feet)

7,400
7,200
7,000
6,800
6,600
6,400
6,200
6,000
5,800
5,600
5,400

San Pedro Creek

Hagan

Coyote

Tonque Pueblo

0 1 2 3 4 5 6 7 8 9 10 11 12 13 14 15 16 17 18 19 20 21 22 23 24

Distance (miles)

Ride Description

Ride northwest, continuing on Puertecito Road, and immediately make a steep descent into an arroyo and the red-rock world of the Chinle Formation. Cross the arroyo and bear left, avoiding private property by staying on the main road. The route traverses the arroyo bottom, passing colorful outcrops of Chinle mudstones with yellow Entrada sandstone above. In a little over a mile the road enters a broad valley, passing the collection of scattered homes known as Puertecito. At a minor intersection, bear right, passing a windmill. As the road crosses a small hill, the ridge to the right offers another look at Chinle and Entrada sandstone. The ridge is broken by a broad fault; look for an offset in the rock layers in the middle of the cliff.

Three miles from the start, turn right at a major intersection. The route now travels across the Chinle valley, climbing in time toward younger rocks. The mesa that dominates the scene to the right of the road at the boundary of the Diamond Tail Ranch is layered with rocks from the Jurassic period and capped with a thick sill of volcanic rock. Ahead, the sill tilts down to road level; the road and San Pedro Creek cut through the sill in a narrow gap four miles from the start.

Once through the gap, the road enters another broad valley, this one on Mancos shale. The next sandstone ridge, about 5.5 miles from the start, is small. Riding through the roadcut, look for chocolate-brown layers of rock. Abundant fossils are found only in this layer. Continue down a small drainage to Arroyo Uña de

Ruins of the Large Company Buildings at Hagan

Gato (Cat's Claw). Suddenly, the ruins of Hagan appear across the wash. Look for the huge company buildings, small houses, and the dumps of the coal mines scattered across the hillsides. Enjoy Hagan from the road—the town itself is on private land.

Past Hagan, the road crosses Arroyo Uña de Gato and passes a few small ruins, outliers of the town. Here the road parallels the railbed of the Rio Grande Eastern Railway, seen to the left. Look for petroglyphs carved in the desert varnish on the tan sandstone cliff to the right. After cutting through a gap in the cliff, the road follows a rolling course to the melting adobes of Coyote, about four miles from Hagan. The former residents of the ghost town selected a picturesque setting for their town. Enjoy the long views to the Jemez Mountains to the west, the Sangre de Cristos to the north, and the sloping east flank of the Sandias to the south.

Beyond Coyote, ride past the Diamond Tail Ranch Headquarters. About a mile from the ranch is a cattle guard and fence line marking the boundary of San Felipe Pueblo lands. Just before the boundary is an extensive cleared area to the left. This is the site of Tonque Pueblo and the Tonque brickworks. From the road, piles of tan bricks and foundations of company buildings can be seen, as can the faint outlines of Tonque Pueblo. To avoid damaging any fragile archeological structures, stay on the road when exploring this area.

Tonque is the turnaround point; return to the car park by the same route. Due to the northern tilt of the rocks, the scenery on the return ride is surprisingly different. From the north, each ridge is approached from its gently sloping, vegetated side, and the ride assumes the character of a trip through rolling hills.

Background

Surrounded by mountains, the Hagan Basin is a huge bowl filled with colorful stories, and even the rocks of the Hagan area have a tale to tell. The story begins thirty million years ago as the Rio Grande rift was formed and the Sandia Mountains were thrust a mile into the air. The surrounding rocks, including those in the Hagan Basin, were tilted and eventually exposed in one of the most complete sections of geologic history found in New Mexico. From the Sandias to the Cerrillos Hills, the sequence of rocks runs from limestones deposited 325 million years ago to mudstones of a relatively young forty million years.

Imagine building a special layered cake. First is a layer of chocolate cake overlaid with a thin band of vanilla icing. Next is another fat layer of cake, this time yellow. Perhaps a coating of strawberry jam is next, followed by layers of more cake, pudding, and finally a thin coat of melted chocolate. For this cake, the bottom layer of chocolate is the "oldest" layer of the dessert, the layer first put in place. Layers become "younger" toward the top, and the "youngest" layer is the melted chocolate deposited last.

So it goes with rocks. Different rock types are laid down in a sequence from oldest to youngest. An ancient sea might leave behind a layer of limestone, which might be followed by sandstones formed from the grains of ancient beaches, then perhaps layers of mudstone, shales, or even lava until the sequence is complete.

A cake will sit in a neat pile of stacked bands. A knife cutting through the cake from the side slices all the layers simultaneously. But suppose a certain two-year-old lunges for the irresistible cake and knocks it askew, creating a slanting pile of layered sugar. In cutting the slanted cake, a knife will cut the bottom, oldest, layer first, then individually through the successive, younger layers.

As in a cake, rock formations are deposited in horizontal layers, but these, too, can be pushed on edge. As the Sandia Mountains were pushed upward, the rocks of the Hagan area were tilted, dipping gently into the ground to the northeast. Like the knife through the knocked-over cake, a mountain bike rider traveling from the Sandias to Tonque encounters the rock layers in sequence from oldest to youngest.

Hop on a two-wheeled time machine and climb through time. The pageant of the rise and fall of ancient oceans is a rare display of geology laid bare for all to see. At the start of the ride, the route drops into a red arroyo in the Chinle Formation. These mudstones were deposited on a broad floodplain, extending eastward from Arizona and Utah at the time of the earliest dinosaurs. Riding north, the route crosses a line of buff-colored cliffs, the Entrada Formation, which was laid down as sand dunes in a huge desert. Atop the Entrada is a gray layer of limestone. This is the Todilto Formation, deposited in a shallow lake that replaced the sand desert. Through the cliffs of hard, resistant rock is another broad valley of mudstones, the Morrison Formation, famous for its abundance of dinosaur fossils. Next is a sequence representing the incursion and regression of a large shallow sea over New

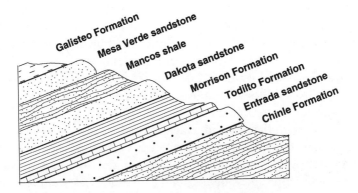

Cross Section of Rocks of the Hagan Basin

Mexico: near-shore Dakota sandstone, off-shore mudstones of the Mancos shale, and off-shore Mesa Verde sandstone. Completing the rock layer cake near Coyote is the Galisteo Formation, deposited on floodplains about forty million years ago.

Among the rocks deposited during the time of the dinosaurs were thin but extensive layers of coal. The discovery of coal seams in the rocks along the Arroyo Uña de Gato led to the formation of the New Mexico Fuel and Iron Company in 1902. By the end of the year, the company opened the Hagan Mine and about sixty workers lived in the village that acquired the same name. Two years later, encouraged by increasing profits, the company opened the Sloan Mine three miles to the west. As more miners worked at the Sloan, the town of Coyote was established near the mine.

Around the same time, another group of investors saw potential in the deep clays along Arroyo Coyote. Purchasing a small parcel of land from the Diamond Tail Ranch, the Albuquerque investors formed the Tonque Pressed Brick, Tile, and Improvement Company. Constructing shops, kilns, and a storehouse, the Tonque Company manufactured bricks on the site from 1912 to 1942. Clay was dug from a huge pit on the banks of the arroyo. Workers from the brick plant lived in either Coyote or Hagan.

Because of the high cost of shipping coal to markets, the mining operations and hence the towns of Hagan and Coyote remained small. Two railroad projects briefly gave the communities hope for a brighter future, but both fell through. Coyote survived for a dozen years as the home of coal miners and brickyard workers, but when the Sloan mine closed in 1923, the town closed with it. A year later, a railroad was finally built up Tonque Arroyo, too late for Coyote, but giving new life to Hagan. The 12.6-mile Rio Grande Eastern Railway Company connected Hagan to the Santa Fe Railroad, allowing larger shipments of coal. The line also carried bricks from the Tonque works.

With the railroad, Hagan experienced a growth spurt. The company built a power plant, maintenance shops and a warehouse. As the population grew to five hundred, the town acquired a hotel and new stores. New owners of the Tonque Brick Company moved their pressing plant five miles up the arroyo to the now thriving town. Hagan enjoyed a six-year period of prosperity.

In 1931, the coal vein at the Hagan mine suddenly pinched out, leaving the owners with no choice but to close the mine. With no freight other than bricks from Tonque, the railroad was soon abandoned. In a few short years, Hagan became the second ghost town on Arroyo Uña de Gato.

Or was Hagan the third ghost town in the Hagan Basin? Tonque Pueblo was a large village of uncertain affiliation near the junction of arroyos Coyote and Tonque. The site was probably selected because of the nearby supply of water, fertile soil, firewood, adobe soil for building material, and clay for pottery. At its height, Tonque was probably home to three thousand people housed in 1,500 to 2,000 living and storage rooms, most built in a single story. The village had an unusual design, consisting of three same-sized parallel buildings with plazas in between. One great kiva, a large, circular ceremonial structure with several distinctive features, is found at the ruin. Available tree-ring dates indicate that some of the construction occurred between the 1430s and 1521, and the presence of Spanish metal objects indicates the pueblo was partially occupied at least until the arrival of Coronado in 1540. The site holds no evidence of disease or of conflict with the Spanish, and abandonment remains a mystery. In fact, there are many signs of a planned evacuation, such as a storage room with fifteen neatly stacked manos and metates.

Today, the valley of the Arroyo Uña de Gato feels truly haunted. The ruins of the immense company buildings at Hagan are impressive. Smaller ruins of houses line the arroyo for half a mile and the slopes above the town are scarred with mines and dumps, all standing in eerie silence. Farther downstream stand a half-dozen melting adobes, all that remains of Coyote. Many signs of the brickworks remain at Tonque: scattered broken bricks, the deep pit from which the clay was taken, and foundations of kilns, shops, and a storehouse are all found near the road. Also at Tonque, in the extensive area of disturbed ground, are the faint outlines of the three clay buildings of the ancient pueblo.

Further Reading

Barnett, Franklin. *Tonque Pueblo*. Albuquerque: Albuquerque Archeological Society, 1969.

Kelley, Vincent C., and S.A. Northrop. *Geology of Sandia Mountains and Vicinity*. Socorro: New Mexico Bureau of Mines and Mineral Resources, 1975.

Sherman, James E., and Barbara H. Sherman. *Ghost Towns and Mining Camps of New Mexico*. Norman: University of Oklahoma Press, 1975.

Varney, Philip. *New Mexico's Best Ghost Towns*. Albuquerque: University of New Mexico Press, 1987.

La Liendre

■ ■ ■ ■ ■ ■ ■ ■ ■ ■ ■ ■ ■ ■ ■ ■ ■ ■ ■

Location: southeast of Las Vegas, New Mexico
Distance: 13 miles
Elevation: 5,700 to 6,800 feet
Elevation Change: 1,100 feet
Skill Level: easy
Seasons: late March to early June, late August to
    October
Ride Surface: paved, gravel, and dirt roads
Interesting Features: ghost town, homestead ruins,
    scenic views, Gallinas River canyon
Map: USGS Apache Springs 15-minute quadrangle

Access

● ● ● ● ● ● ● ● ● ● ● ● ● ● ● ● ● ●

From I-25 in Las Vegas, take NM 104 at exit 345. Head east, away from Las Vegas, toward Conchas Lake and Tucumcari. After 7.5 miles of rolling across the Great Plains, turn right at the intersection with NM 67. In a little more than six miles, follow the road as it jogs left. At 7.5 miles from NM 104, park at a broad gravel area on the right, which is just before the road begins to descend a steep hill.

LA LIENDRE

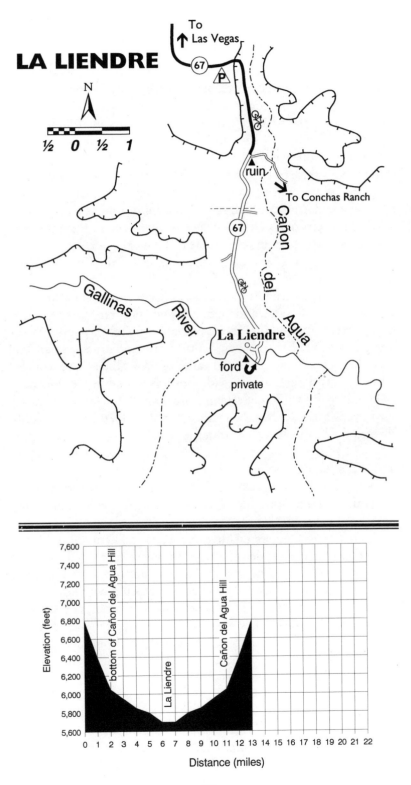

Ride Description

━ ━ ━ ━ ━ ━ ━ ━ ━ ━ ━

Mountain biking on a state highway is not usually recommended, but NM 67 is an exception. As this ride begins from the gravel car park at the edge of a huge expanse of grass, the route is paved. Follow the road as it turns sharply south and quickly descends, clinging to a narrow shelf above the Cañon del Agua. Over the next two miles, the road drops eight hundred feet to near the canyon bottom. Cruise down the hill, enjoying the ever-widening views of below-the-rim country to the south. At two miles the pavement ends and the road splits. Continue straight on NM 67, passing the left fork signed for the Conchas Ranch. Just past the intersection are the ruins of a stone cabin on the left.

The route is now below the caprock, in the Ceja, and the scene in all directions is one of broad valleys and striped mesas. Over the next two miles the road surface is variously attired in pavement, gravel, sand, and mud. Near milepost ten, pass through a large steel gate (be sure to close it after riding through). After milepost twelve, pass through another gate and cross a small arroyo. In another mile, the broad valley of the Gallinas River comes into view. At a bend in the road, look for a large stone ruin surrounded by the withering remains of an apple orchard. The next turn opens a view down the main street of La Liendre. Bear right toward the large ruins seen from the road.

La Liendre is a magical old place, perched on a low bluff above the flowing Gallinas River and its attendant large cottonwoods, with colorful rocks in all directions. Feel free to explore the entire town by foot, but do not enter any of the buildings, for personal safety, and for their protection. A few structures, some stone and frame, others melting adobe, are still standing. Many more buildings can be identified as such only by the broken rubble of their foundations. The largest ruin, perhaps the post office and general store, is equipped with a cellar. A stroll down the street is like piecing together a jigsaw puzzle, using the outlines of walls to reconstruct the appearance of the village and the function of each structure. Enjoy the view of the Gallinas Valley from the west end of La Liendre, but respect the unfriendly fence that encloses a few buildings farther down the river bluff.

A few hundred feet farther down the road, NM 67 leads to a ford of the Gallinas River. Ride to the ford and look across the river into a grove of cottonwoods for the ruins of what must be a part of the Cabeza de Baca hacienda. Fenced private property begins just beyond the river, so the ford makes a good turnaround point. Before heading back, enjoy the shade of the cottonwoods at the base of the river bluff. Return to the car park by the same route. The long climb up Cañon del Agua Hill is smooth and gentle, an enjoyable conclusion to the ride.

Background

Throughout most of the Rocky Mountain West, the term *ghost town* is synonymous with mining town. However, in an arid land where agriculture must rely on dependable summer rainfall that often does not come, farming and ranching communities, too, frequently wither away.

Near Las Vegas, New Mexico, the endless grass of the Great Plains spreads eastward like an ocean from the foot of the Sangre de Cristo Mountains; the great Llano country extends from the mountains into eastern Texas. In spite of the seeming monotony of the landscape, just southeast of Las Vegas, the Llano is broken by deep canyons carved by the Gallinas River and its small tributaries. Below the caprock of the canyons is the Ceja, the "eyebrow," of the plains. The streams and rivers that flow through the Ceja provide more water than is available on the plains above. Drawn by water, the buffalo who roamed the canyons, and the excellent grazing lands, early settlers came to the Ceja to establish their ranches.

Below the caprock south of Las Vegas, La Liendre was one of several ranching communities established along the Gallinas River. The town was settled between 1845 and 1850 by Juan de Dios Maes and a family named Duran. Attracted by the rich bottomlands of the Gallinas and the infinite grazing lands of the plains, the families adopted a difficult lifestyle of raising beans and corn in the valley, and grazing sheep and horses in the grasslands. A few years later, these first families were joined by the Cabeza de Baca family, who established the headquarters of their extensive ranch just across the river from La Liendre.

The Cabeza de Baca Ranch employed a large number of sheepherders and ranch hands. Employees brought their families to the Ceja, and most settled in La Liendre. Houses were built close together for protection from the real threat of the Plains Indians. Local adobe and stone were used as building material. As more houses were added to the community, they spread along the river bluff in a single line. The view of the bluff from across the river gave the town its name: La Liendre translates to "a string of nits." The town acquired a post office in 1878. Its tenuous link with the outside world was made stronger in 1912 when the hazardous route down Gallinas Canyon was abandoned after the state of New Mexico built a modern road down Cañon del Agua Hill.

Sheep were the primary livestock on the Ceja until the 1890s when cattle raising became dominant. Homesteaders and long droughts made life on the Ceja difficult on the Cabeza de Baca Ranch and in La Liendre. Most of the ranchers were driven out during the Dust Bowl years of the early 1930s. Enough families remained in La Liendre to maintain the post office until the 1940s, but shortly after the Second World War the town was completely abandoned.

The remains of La Liendre are spread along a half-mile of river bluff. Many foundations of barns, corrals, homes and the post office remain, but the town is quickly deteriorating, probably due more to vandalism than decay. In 1964, Betty Woods wrote of houses with broken windows and swinging doors, a fading sign identifying the post office, and even a mailbox still standing. Philip Varney's photographs, taken in the late 1970s, show an almost complete roof on the largest building. Today, none of these features remains, and only three collapsing buildings—two homes and a store—still rise above their foundations.

The Remains of the General Store at La Liendre

Further Reading

Cabeza de Baca, Fabiola. *We Fed Them Cactus*. Albuquerque: University of New Mexico Press, 1954.

Varney, Philip. *New Mexico's Best Ghost Towns*. Albuquerque: University of New Mexico Press, 1987.

Woods, Betty. *Ghost Towns of New Mexico and How to Get to Them*. Santa Fe: Sunstone Press, 1964.

Chapter 3
Where's Waldo?
■■■■■■■■■■■■■■■■■■■■■■■

Location: between Santa Fe and Albuquerque
Distance: 16 miles
Elevation: 5,600 to 6,150 feet
Elevation Change: 900 feet
Skill Level: easy
Seasons: muddy after winter snows, hot in summer; best late fall through early spring
Ride Surface: gravel road
Interesting Features: ghost towns, mines, fossils
Maps: USGS Madrid and Tetilla Peak 7.5-minute quadrangles

Access
● ● ● ● ● ● ● ● ● ● ● ● ● ● ● ● ● ●

From Santa Fe, take I-25 south about fourteen miles to exit 267; from Albuquerque, exit 267 is about forty-five miles north. This exit is not marked, nor are there signs warning of its approach; watch the mileposts to know when it is near. Exit the interstate and head east, crossing the frontage road. Park just beyond a fence near a sign pointing toward Waldo and Los Cerrillos.

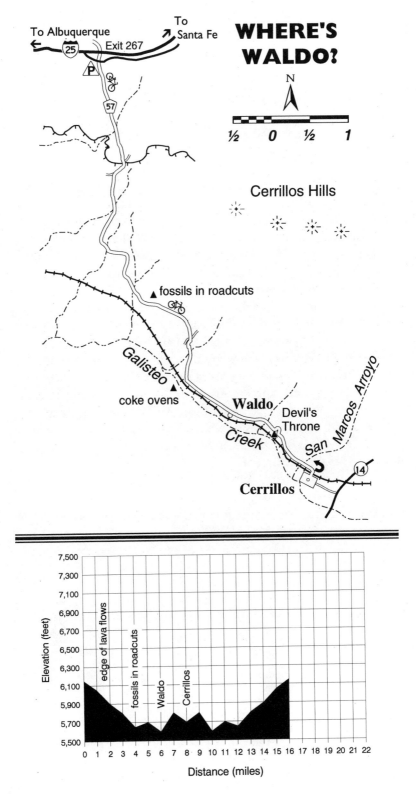

WHERE'S WALDO?

To Albuquerque
To Santa Fe
Exit 267
25
57

N

½ 0 ½ 1

Cerrillos Hills

▲ fossils in roadcuts

Galisteo

coke ovens ▲

Waldo
Devil's
Throne

Creek

San Marcos Arroyo

Cerrillos

14

Elevation profile:

Elevation (feet): 7,500 / 7,300 / 7,100 / 6,900 / 6,700 / 6,500 / 6,300 / 6,100 / 5,900 / 5,700 / 5,500

edge of lava flows
fossils in roadcuts
Waldo
Cerrillos

Distance (miles): 0 1 2 3 4 5 6 7 8 9 10 11 12 13 14 15 16 17 18 19 20 21 22

Chapter 3

Ride Description
▬ ▬ ▬ ▬ ▬ ▬ ▬ ▬ ▬ ▬

As a mid-winter or early spring ride, this route is a perfect cure for cabin fever, without taxing the legs or lungs too much. With fossils, a ghost town, and an old town that refuses to become a ghost, pedaling to Waldo and Los Cerrillos makes an ideal family ride.

Begin riding on the gravel road to Cerrillos, Santa Fe County Road 57, on top of a basalt mesa. The source of the lava is the rounded hill on the other side of the interstate. The Cerrillos Hills are to the east. Enjoy the grasslands dotted with junipers, and listen for the lilting sounds of the song of the abundant meadowlarks on the fence posts. In about 1.5 miles, descend from the eastern edge of the lava flows and enter a small canyon with walls composed of sandstones and mudstones. For the next three miles, continue a gradual descent. As you follow the winding road across the low hills, inspect the yellowish-gray roadcuts because fossils are common in the shales. Look for spiral shells, small clam-like shells, and long tubes, which are the remains of worm burrows.

Five-and-a-half miles from the start, the road turns to parallel Galisteo Creek and the Atchison, Topeka and Santa Fe Railroad to the right. Look across the railroad tracks and the wash for the extensive foundations of coke ovens built around the turn of the century. In another half-mile, a small cluster of cottonwood trees marks the location of Waldo. Only a few foundations remain here at the town site. A mile past Waldo, climb steeply around the dramatic Devil's Throne, a mass of magma that cooled and hardened before it reached the surface. On the other side, ride a steep descent, then continue a half-mile to San Marcos Arroyo (do not enter if flooded). Drop into and out of the arroyo, cross a cattle guard, then turn right into Cerrillos on the first road that crosses the railroad tracks.

Slowly ride into Cerrillos, enter the trees, and be transported into a different world. Tour the unpaved streets of the town, looking for the Clear Light Opera House, the two old hotels, the rustic church, and the "scenic view."

To return to the car park, ride to the main intersection in Cerrillos at the "Murphy-Dolan Store." Ride north past a modern general store, cross the railroad tracks and turn left onto Santa Fe County Road 57. Return past San Marcos Arroyo, the Devil's Throne, and Waldo, finishing with a gradual climb back to the top of the lava flows near the interstate.

Background

The most ancient mines in the southwest are the turquoise workings at Mount Chalchihuitl in the Cerrillos Hills. The precious stone was dug out of the rock by miners from the Rio Grande pueblos and their Anasazi ancestors, perhaps as early as 500 A.D. At the site is a pit between 25 and 130 feet deep and 250 feet across. As much as one hundred thousand cubic yards of earth may have been moved by hand. Mining was done with stone tools, and by heating the rocks and dousing them with cold water, causing them to shatter.

The Spanish discovered the riches of the Cerrillos Hills as early as 1582. Miners from Santa Fe reopened the ancient turquoise pit and established underground workings at the Mina de Tiro, the "Mine of the Shaft." Using slave labor from the pueblos, gold, silver and turquoise were removed. In 1680, an underground cave-in killed twenty slaves and may have contributed to unrest that led to the Pueblo Revolt, which drove the Spanish from New Mexico for a dozen years.

Modern mining in the Cerrillos Hills began with the discovery of silver and zinc ores in 1879. Inspired perhaps by stories of ancient Spanish gold mines, miners from Colorado combed the Cerrillos Hills and found rich ore in several locations. Almost overnight, three towns rose near the richest strikes: Bonanza City was

Cabins and Mines at Cerrillos, New Mexico, ca. 1884.
(Photograph by J.R. Riddle, Courtesy, Museum of New Mexico, Santa Fe, Negative No. 76116.)

founded at the base of the hill with the same name; five miles south, the town first known as Carbonateville, then Turquesa, was born; and Cerrillos, the most lasting community, found life along Galisteo Creek.

By mid-summer 1879, three hundred miners worked the hills above the tent camp of Cerrillos, filing over one thousand mining claims. Prospectors found veins of gold, silver, copper, lead and zinc; some worked the old turquoise mines. Although Bonanza and Carbonateville boomed and died within a few short years, the arrival of the Atchison, Topeka and Santa Fe Railroad at Cerrillos in 1880 brought the camp at least some hope of permanence.

With so much wealth in the rocks, Santa Fe businessmen opened branch stores in Cerrillos, and the railroad built Los Cerrillos Station. When coal was discovered in nearby Madrid Gulch, Cerrillos became the supply center for the surrounding mining districts. By its peak of activity in 1890, Cerrillos had a thriving population of two thousand.

By 1891, most of the precious metal mining in the Cerrillos Hills was finished; but there was always a trickle of ore coming in from the hills—just enough to keep Cerrillos alive. Turquoise mining by New York jewelry firms created a minor boom in the late 1890s. Coal mining in the gulches to the south helped keep the town's people employed. From 1900 to 1950, sporadic activity at twelve different mines held a small population in Cerrillos. As late as 1959, the discovery of a previously unknown copper deposit gave new hope to the town, but the ore body proved too small and low grade for profitable mining. Today, the few people who remain in Cerrillos work the tourist trade, do small-scale mining in the hills above town, or commute to jobs in Santa Fe.

The charm of Cerrillos endures, not only for tourists but for Hollywood. In the late fifties, Walt Disney Studios used Cerrillos as the backdrop for a film about the bandit Elfego Baca. Recently, the town received a new coat of paint for the movie *Young Guns*. As it was in the movie, the old hotel on the corner of Main Street is still identified as the "Murphy-Dolan Store."

Coal and the railroad also gave life to Waldo. The town was established as a railroad stop in 1880. Waldo led a quiet existence until 1892 when a spur line was built to the extensive coal mines in Madrid, and the town found new life in shipping supplies, including 150,000 gallons of water per day, to the mines. Waldo expanded again when the Colorado Fuel and Iron Company established a coke processing plant a half-mile west of town. The company built fifteen coke ovens on the south bank of Galisteo

Creek and produced high-grade smelting coke. By 1921, over a hundred residents lived under the cottonwoods along the railroad tracks.

After diesel fuel replaced coal as the main power for the railroads, mining at Madrid declined. When the mines closed in 1954, Waldo, entirely dependent on Madrid for its business, became a ghost town.

Further Reading

Disbrow, Alan E., and Walter Stoll. *Geology of the Cerrillos Area, Santa Fe County, New Mexico*. New Mexico Bureau of Mines and Mineral Resources Bulletin 48. Socorro: New Mexico Bureau of Mines and Mineral Resources, 1957.

Lawson, Jacqueline E. *Cerrillos: Yesterday, Today, and Tomorrow*. Santa Fe: Sunstone Press, 1989.

Cabezon

■ ■ ■ ■ ■ ■ ■ ■ ■ ■ ■ ■ ■ ■ ■ ■ ■

Location: northwest of Albuquerque
Distance: 26 miles
Elevation: 5,900 to 6,500 feet
Elevation Change: 1,200 feet
Skill Level: moderate
Seasons: October to May, except following winter
   snows
Ride Surface: gravel and dirt roads
Interesting Features: ghost town, volcanic necks,
   evidence of severe erosion, solitude
Maps: USGS Cabezon and San Luis 7.5-minute
   quadrangles

Access

● ● ● ● ● ● ● ● ● ● ● ● ● ● ● ● ●

From San Ysidro, take NM 44 north toward Cuba. Eighteen miles from San Ysidro, turn left onto a gravel road marked for San Luis and Cabezon. (From Cuba, this road is twenty-two miles south on NM 44.) Travel about ten miles on the gravel and dirt road, through the village of San Luis to a dirt road coming in from the left (east) near a pipeline. Park along the road in any of the wide turnouts.

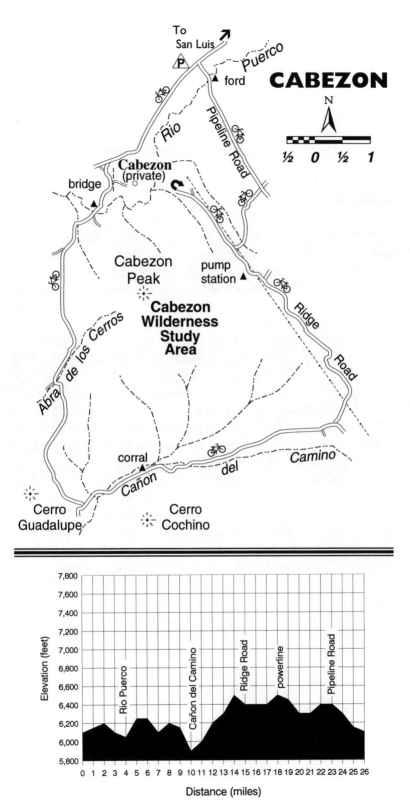

CABEZON

To San Luis

P

Puerco

ford

N

½ 0 ½ 1

Rio

Pipeline Road

Cabezon (private)

bridge

Cabezon Peak

pump station

Cabezon Wilderness Study Area

Abra de los Cerros

Ridge Road

corral

Cañon   del   Camino

Cerro Guadalupe

Cerro Cochino

Elevation (feet)

7,800
7,600
7,400
7,200
7,000
6,800
6,600
6,400
6,200
6,000
5,800

Rio Puerco

Cañon del Camino

Ridge Road

powerline

Pipeline Road

0 1 2 3 4 5 6 7 8 9 10 11 12 13 14 15 16 17 18 19 20 21 22 23 24 25 26

Distance (miles)

Ride Description

━━━━━━━━━━━━

The Cabezon Loop is a scenic ride made difficult only by its length. The grades are easy, and, if dry, the road surface is packed and non-technical. The route is through open grasslands with scattered juniper and piñon pines, and shade is scarce; this is not a summer ride. The entire loop is dominated by the volcanic massif of Cabezon Peak. As the route circles around the old volcano, the peak is visible from almost every point.

On the loop, riders must twice cross the Rio Puerco. The first crossing is over a bridge. At this point, note the condition of the river below. The second crossing is a concrete ford that should not be attempted under flood conditions, which are most likely to occur after heavy summer thunderstorms. If the stream under the bridge is running high, do not attempt the loop ride, but consider riding out to Cañon del Camino and back.

The loop encloses the Bureau of Land Management's Cabezon Wilderness Study Area (WSA). The roads within the WSA are closed to all but foot travel, and mountain bike riders should stay on the described route, which closely parallels the WSA boundary. Note that much of the land around the village of Cabezon is private. Because of past experiences with looters, the owners of the village don't take kindly to trespassers. Be watchful of fence lines, and always obey "No Trespassing" signs.

Begin riding south toward Cabezon on the San Luis road. The route climbs slowly for 2.5 miles to an intersection near the top of a hill. Turn left, and descend rapidly toward the Rio Puerco bridge. The first view of the village of Cabezon is just before the Rio Puerco bridge; look left where a fence parallels the road. At the bridge over the Rio Puerco, stop to observe the patterns of erosion. The deeply incised arroyo did not exist before 1880—an astonishing rate of downcutting in only one hundred years!

Beyond the bridge, climb to the benches above the Puerco as Cabezon Peak looms to the left. At the top of a short, steep grade above the Rio Puerco Valley, the road cuts through an interesting ledge of Dakota sandstone, and the suddenly expansive view is filled with many volcanic necks, both sharp-ridged and rounded. One mile after reaching the bench level, begin a descent through terrain crisscrossed with more signs of the severe impact of overgrazing in the form of deep, narrow arroyos. With Cerro Guadalupe dead ahead, descend along the Abra de los Cerros for about a mile to a Y-intersection. Turn left, and climb to a low knoll. At the top,

Cerro Guadalupe dominates the western view. Although Cabezon Peak is more imposing, Cerro Guadalupe exhibits finer sculpturing; the basalt congealed in this volcano forms spires, towers, and turrets.

Begin a fun descent to Cañon del Camino. While riding parallel to Cerro Guadalupe, the view encompasses the Rio Puerco Valley, Mesa Prieta, and Cerro de Nuestra Señora, another massive neck sixteen miles south. Near the bottom of the cañon, turn left on the road heading up the drainage. Pedaling up the gentle hill, yellow cliffs of Mancos shale are on the left, and the base of Cerro Cochino is on the right. A mile up Cañon del Camino are a corral and gate. Pass through the gate (be sure to close it behind you) and continue the gentle climb. One-and-a-half miles beyond the corral, the road climbs sharply to the top of a ridge where Cabezon Peak and the Jemez Mountains are in view. After two miles along the ridgetop, cross a cattle guard and turn left, riding toward a powerline to the northeast. Ride this road, the BLM's Ridge Road 1113, crossing under the powerline and continuing along the ridgetop.

After riding about 3.5 miles on Ridge Road, turn onto a track to the left, riding toward the powerline and climbing a steep, rocky hill. At the top, cross under the powerline and ride by a half-buried pump station. Continue as the road turns northwest, dropping gradually. A half-mile from the top, note a side road dropping off to the right: this is the route out. Proceed down the hill parallel to the powerline to a fork about two miles from the pump station. Take the left fork, dropping down a steep and rocky drainage. Soon the village of Cabezon comes into view. Binoculars will provide a closer look at the buildings on private land across the Rio Puerco. Avoid trespassing by turning around before reaching the floodplain of the river.

After viewing the village of Cabezon, return uphill about two miles to the road that drops off the ridge a half-mile below the pump station. Follow this road for 1.5 miles to a four-way intersection with Ridge Road and a pipeline road. Turn left onto the pipeline road, dropping in two miles to the Rio Puerco. Cross the muddy stream at the concrete ford, and complete the loop in one mile.

Background

Cabezon (large head) Peak is the dominant feature of the landscape of the middle Rio Puerco Valley, rising over two thousand feet above the surrounding plain and visible from fifty miles away in any direction. Such a landmark usually figures in the legends of Native Americans, and Cabezon is a sacred peak to both Jemez Pueblo and the Navajos. To the Navajos, Cabezon is Tsenajn—Black Peak—one of the four mountains marking the boundary of their world. The peak represents the head of a giant killed by the Twin Brothers; the hardened lava at the base is the giant's congealed blood.

Cabezon Peak is the most prominent of dozens of volcanic necks between the Jemez Mountains and Mount Taylor. Each spire of dark rock represents the site of volcanic eruptions. A volcanic neck is formed when magma, melted rock within the earth's crust, rises toward the surface but cools and hardens in the throat of the volcano before flowing out onto the land. Solidified lava is

Cabezon Peak, a Massive Volcanic Neck along the Rio Puerco

usually harder than the surrounding rock, so as erosion strips away the land, the more resistant lava erodes more slowly, eventually standing higher than the surrounding plain.

In the early nineteenth century, the rich grazing land of the Rio Puerco Valley attracted many Spanish settlers. Cabezon town was one of a half-dozen settlements scattered along the river. Lured by water for easy irrigation, the settlers built homes and farms wherever the topography permitted planting crops along the river.

Land grants to the Maestas and Montoya families in the 1760s began the documented history of settlement in the town of Cabezon. Living within the world of the Navajo proved difficult, and the ranches were abandoned and resettled at least twice between 1774 and 1872. Reports by the Spanish explorers Dominguez and Escalante in 1776 and the American James Abert in 1846 comment on the evidence of settlement along the Rio Puerco at the foot of Cabezon Peak.

After the Navajos were forced onto their reservation in 1868, descendants of the original Spanish families moved back to Cabezon. They farmed along the river and herded cattle and sheep on the surrounding range. The river ford just east of town on the ancient Jemez-Zuñi Trail became a crossing for the supply route between Santa Fe and Fort Wingate, and in 1875 the town became a stage stop for travellers crossing New Mexico.

By 1880, about ten thousand acres of bottomland in the middle Rio Puerco Valley were under irrigation, and as many as eighty thousand sheep and unnumbered cattle grazed on community ranges in the watershed. The people of the valley experienced relative prosperity, but trouble was on the way. Without realizing the source of the problem, the farmers and ranchers changed the nature of the watershed. Overgrazing by too many hoofed animals stripped the land of gramma grass, leaving snakeweed to take over the range. Stock trails channeled heavy rains into torrents, carving out steep-sided arroyos on mountain slopes and in the flat bottomlands. The weak structure and high solubility of the soils in the Puerco watershed allowed for its easy erosion: over a billion cubic yards of soil have been washed from the watershed since 1885.

Increased runoff from the clearcut headwaters and from the vegetation-stripped rangelands was channeled into the Rio Puerco, causing the river to cut a deep arroyo in the once flat and fertile bottomlands. The river now flowed at the bottom of the arroyo, making it impossible to remove water for irrigation, and lowering the watertable, which also affected "dryland" crops. Without water for crops, and with the rangeland stripped of vegetation, many long-time residents were forced to leave. By 1924, less than three thousand acres in the Rio Puerco Valley were still used for farming.

Though always home to a few residents, by 1954 Cabezon was described as a ghost town. Formerly the owners opened the town to tourists, but thoughtless visitors destroyed or carried away many of the remaining artifacts. Now Cabezon is posted, and the owners will not tolerate trespassers.

Stories of the old way of life along the Rio Puerco are captured in a poignant book by Narciso Garcia, *Abuelitos: Stories of the Rio Puerco*. Told in both Spanish and English, the tales describe the simple joys and hardships of those living in the Rio Puerco Valley during the early twentieth century. The haunting ghost stories should be read the night before riding the Cabezon Loop.

Further Reading

DuBuys, William. *Enchantment and Exploitation.* Albuquerque: University of New Mexico Press, 1988.

Garcia, Narciso. *Abuelitos: Stories of the Rio Puerco.* Albuquerque: University of New Mexico Press, 1987.

Rittenhouse, Jack. *Cabezon, A New Mexico Ghost Town.* Santa Fe: Stagecoach Press, 1965.

Midnight, Anchor, and La Belle

■■■■■■■■■■■■■■■■■■■■■■■■■■■

Location: north of Red River, Sangre de Cristo
　　　Mountains, Carson National Forest
Distance: 6 miles
Elevation: 10,400 to 10,800 feet
Elevation Change: 500 feet
Skill Level: easy
Seasons: mid-July to late September
Ride Surface: gravel roads
Interesting Features: ghost towns, mining relics, high
　　　country riding, gold panning
Maps: Carson National Forest, USGS Comanche
　　　Point 7.5-minute quadrangle

Access

● ● ● ● ● ● ● ● ● ● ● ● ● ● ● ● ●

　　From the town of Red River, take FR 597, Mallette Street, north from town up Mallette Creek and over Sawmill Mountain. This well-graded gravel road can easily be traveled by any vehicle. About eleven miles from Red River, turn right at the junction with FR 134. (This point can also be reached from Taos by taking NM 150-522 to Questa, then following FR 134 along Cabresto Creek for ten miles.) Continue up FR 134 about seven miles toward Lagunita Saddle. Pass the junction with FR 54, which is signed for Greenie Peak and Sawmill Canyon. One-quarter mile past FR 54, park at the Y-intersection at Lagunita Saddle.

MIDNIGHT, ANCHOR, AND LA BELLE

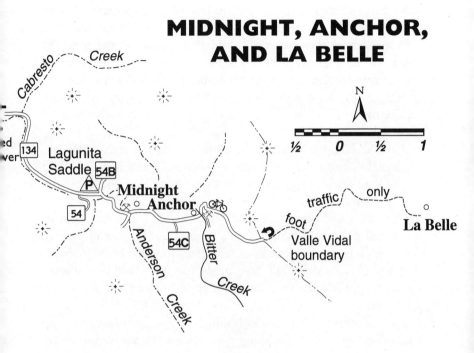

N

½ 0 ½ 1

Cabresto Creek

134
Lagunita
Saddle 54B
P
**Midnight
Anchor**
54
54C
Anderson Creek
Bitter Creek
traffic only
foot
Valle Vidal
boundary
La Belle

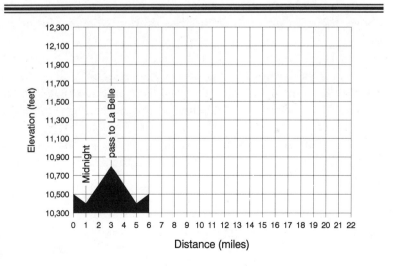

Ride Description

▬ ▬ ▬ ▬ ▬ ▬ ▬ ▬ ▬ ▬ ▬

The ride to Midnight and Anchor is the best family ride in this book. With easy grades (except two very short stretches) and a short total distance, this route can be ridden by anyone. The high meadow scenery is terrific, and youngsters and the young at heart will love to explore the cabins and mine dumps along the way, and to try their hand at gold panning. There is even a chance of seeing working cowboys or a rambling black bear. If the climb on the road to La Belle is too tough, the old road makes a great short hike.

At Lagunita Saddle, begin riding on the right fork and immediately cross the headwaters of Bitter Creek. Quickly climb out of the meadow and into a short stretch of open forest. As the road enters the meadow surrounding Anderson Creek, look to the left for the ruins of a large cabin. This valley is the site of Midnight and once held many cabins, a few businesses, and a small stamp mill. In another few hundred yards, turn left at the intersection and climb a short hill. Stop at the top of the hill and explore the Midnight Mine dump and more ruined cabins of the town of Midnight.

After rambling around Midnight, continue on the road into the woods, gradually dropping into another meadow. Soon after passing a side road marked FR 54C, the route comes to a well-preserved cabin perched on the slope above Bitter Creek. The road turns left and steeply descends to a small flat with the ruins of more cabins, which are all that remain of the town of Anchor. At the bottom of the hill, bear right and drop to the creek. Cross the stream to the headframe of the Anchor Mine, and, on the slope above, the deep pit of the mine. Use caution when exploring in this area.

From the crossing of Bitter Creek, bear left and follow the old road from Anchor to La Belle as it climbs a rocky slope, passing another mine opening on the way. Ride past a vehicle barrier, then enjoy a one-mile gradual climb through aspen groves to the saddle between the two abandoned camps. Stop at the fence along the ridge. The fence marks the boundary of the Valle Vidal section of Carson National Forest; the road from the pass to La Belle is closed except to foot traffic.

Turn around and return to Bitter Creek on the old road. The Anchor area makes an excellent lunch stop and provides the opportunity to try panning for gold in the stream gravels below the mine. From Anchor, return to the car park by the same route.

Riders can extend this trip in four ways. The easiest extension is to begin the ride farther down Cabresto Creek on FR 134. To explore another ghost town, take the six-mile round-trip hike on foot to La Belle from the saddle between Anchor and La Belle. Many jeep roads are located in the area and are shown on the Comanche Creek quadrangle map. For a challenging mountain bike ride, treat this trip as a short spur off Hayenga and Shaw's "Midnight Meadows" ride found in their *The New Mexico Mountain Bike Guide.*

Background

Although not known for an abundance of minerals, the Sangre de Cristo Mountains hold a surprising number of almost vanished mining camps. Within a fifteen-mile radius of the town of Red River are no fewer than twenty such places, each born in a frenzy and living a short, exuberant life. Each camp held sway for a few productive months or years, then quickly faded from memory.

In the mid-1890s, when gold fever again reached a peak in the mountains of northern New Mexico, the toast of the Sangre de Cristos was the isolated town of La Belle. Located on the hills overlooking Comanche Creek in what is now known as Valle Vidal, La Belle was the largest camp in the northern Sangre de Cristos and was the center of activity for all the small towns in the area.

Much of the mountains north of Red River were located within the boundaries of the Sangre de Cristo Grant and under strict control of the United States Freehold Land and Emigration Company. Although a few prospectors made mineral discoveries on the grant, the company did not welcome the intruders. When slumping economic conditions during the early 1890s turned the trickle of gold seekers into a flood, the company had little choice but to open its boundaries to prospectors—for a price, of course.

Led by Ira Wing, hardy prospectors discovered a placer bed along Comanche Creek during the dead of winter in 1894. Soon they had located the source about two miles up Spring (now La Belle) Creek. Word of the find leaked to the rest of the world, and the rush was on. By summer, a town had grown up on the grassy hills, boasting one hundred cabins, two hotels, stores and saloons, and six hundred residents; by December, one hundred claims had been filed, and La Belle's newspaper, the *Cresset,* was printing stories about the town and its happenings.

Proof of La Belle's growing importance is how quickly the rest of the world sought contact with the new community. Within a year, roads were built to La Belle from the railhead at Catskill, up Cabresto Creek from Questa, and up Costilla Canyon to connect with the railroad at Antonito. With good roads and the promise of fortunes to be made, La Belle continued to grow. By July 1895 the mining camp had a population of one thousand and streets complete with eight general stores, doctors, an opera house, a bookshop, shoe and drug stores, a jail, a school, and two sawmills.

New groups of miners combing the mountains grew restive of the United States Freehold Land and Emigration Company's policy requiring a stiff fee for mineral exploration on the Sangre de Cristo Grant. Just outside the grant's boundaries on the upper headwaters of Bitter Creek, a group of prospectors located some color and established a mining district. Sensing regulation-free digging, miners poured into the new Keystone district and quickly located many promising mines. To accommodate the influx of miners, five town sites were laid out in April 1895. Only two survived the summer, the towns of Midnight and Anchor, both named for major mines in the district.

Problems beset the Keystone mines almost immediately. A shortage of water shut down most mining operations for the summer. The low-grade ores found in the mines would not pay for their transportation out of the high valleys for processing. Midnight and Anchor, as well as La Belle, were in desperate need of a

Miner's Cabin above Anchor

mill. Nonetheless, it is hard to resist the lure of gold when it is plainly visible in the rocks and streams. Miners continued to stockpile ores, keeping the camps alive throughout the winter. By 1897, though Anchor had faded, Midnight supported a post office, boarding house, general store, and a population of about two hundred.

La Belle was only four miles over the mountains from Anchor. Mining and other supplies came over the road from La Belle to the Keystone camps, and a stage line brought mail and passengers over the pass three times a week. Miners from the smaller camps followed the "Saturday Night" road over the ridge to partake of the delights of the comparatively cosmopolitan larger town. As mining camps go, La Belle was a peaceful place. Drinking, brawling, and visits to the red-light district did occur, but many of the town's activities were of a family nature: baseball games, boxing matches, foot races and chaperoned Saturday night dances.

After two years of hanging on as best they could, the hopes of those living in the Keystone camps were raised when the Midnight Mine was leased to a group of investors who financed more digging and uncovered ore rich enough to warrant the construction of a small mill. However, as was often the case with small mining operations, when the mill was completed, the money ran out. Later that year, new operators found that the extent of the rich ore was limited, and the mill was again shut down.

La Belle's fade into oblivion began as the ores of the larger mines played out in 1896. A year later, the town was half its peak size; by 1900, only forty-nine hangers-on were left. By then, both Midnight and Anchor were completely deserted, abandoned almost overnight after the closing of the mines.

Further Reading

Hayenga, Brant, and Chris Shaw. *The New Mexico Mountain Bike Guide.* Albuquerque: Big Ring Press, 1991.

Pearson, Jim Berry. *The Red River–Twining Area: A New Mexico Mining Story.* Albuquerque: University of New Mexico Press, 1986.

Red River Pass and the Big Ditch

■■■■■■■■■■■■■■■■■■■■■■■■■■■■■■ ■■

Location: south of Red River, Sangre de Cristo
Mountains, Carson National Forest
Distance: 12 miles
Elevation: 8,800 to 9,900 feet
Elevation Change: 1,100 feet
Skill Level: moderate
Seasons: July through September
Ride Surface: gravel and dirt roads
Interesting Features: the Big Ditch, historic road,
mountain scenery
Maps: Carson National Forest, USGS Red River and
Red River Pass 7.5-minute quadrangles

Access

●●●●●●●●●●●●●●●●●●

From the east end of the town of Red River on NM 38,
turn right onto NM 578. Drive 1.3 miles to FR 488, a gravel road
coming in from the left. Park at the intersection.

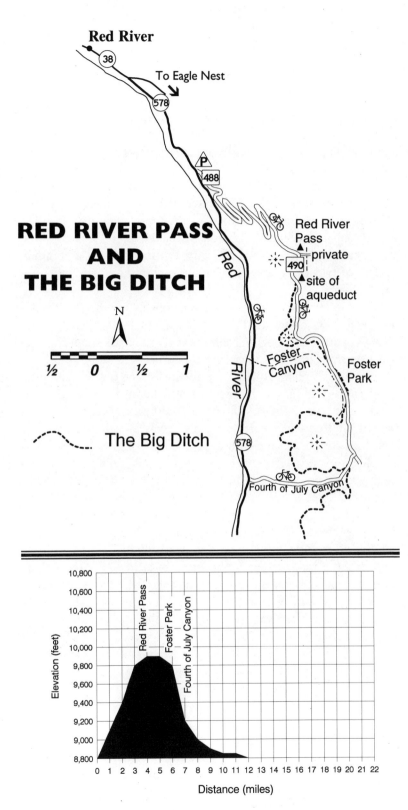

RED RIVER PASS AND THE BIG DITCH

Red River

38

To Eagle Nest

578

P 488

Red River

Red River Pass

private

490

site of aqueduct

River

Foster Canyon

Foster Park

578

Fourth of July Canyon

N

½ 0 ½ 1

- - - The Big Ditch

Elevation (feet)

10,800
10,600
10,400
10,200
10,000
9,800
9,600
9,400
9,200
9,000
8,800

Red River Pass

Foster Park

Fourth of July Canyon

0 1 2 3 4 5 6 7 8 9 10 11 12 13 14 15 16 17 18 19 20 21 22

Distance (miles)

Ride Description

▬ ▬ ▬ ▬ ▬ ▬ ▬ ▬ ▬ ▬ ▬

Begin pedaling up FR 488. No warm-up here: the climb begins immediately and continues for the next four miles. However, the engineers who designed and built this road eighty years ago did a marvelous job, and the grade is never steep, even when swinging around the six switchbacks.

During the first half-mile, ride past outcrops of hydrothermally altered rocks. The distinctive yellow, orange, brown and purple colors keyed early miners to the presence of metals in the Red River area. Mineralization is visible in the rocks at the first switchback, where crystals of shiny, tan orthoclase—a common variety of feldspar made of potassium, aluminum, and silicon—can be found.

On the way to the second switchback, the modern road is visible straight down the hillside. (Those with excellent eyesight or a passion for fishing will also spot trout in the small lake below.) As the climb continues, the views become more grand, encompassing Elephant Rock to the northwest and the Wheeler Peak Wilderness to the south. By the fourth switchback, the folds of the road can be seen below as they wind up the steep slope.

At Red River Pass, it hardly seems like the summit of a four-mile, one-thousand-foot climb. Indeed, the easy portion of the ride is over; several short but steep sections follow. Turn right at the fence onto FR 490 heading south toward Fourth of July Canyon. Make a steep climb followed by a steeper descent. A quarter-mile from the pass, a small pond at the bottom of another hill marks where the Big Ditch crossed the divide and dropped from the Red River side into the Moreno watershed.

After more steep climbs and rapid drops, the road clings to a narrow, rocky shelf overlooking the Red River Canyon. At the start of the next climb, the Big Ditch is clearly visible to the right. This is a good spot to stop and walk along the ditch for a short distance to view its construction. About 5.5 miles from the start, the road enters Foster Park, a long meadow. Halfway through the park, the Big Ditch appears on the left side of the road. While riding along the ditch for one hundred yards, it is not easy to picture this ugly little trench as a marvel of engineering.

Cross the ditch where the road begins to climb out of Foster Park. A half-mile from the park, a Y-intersection at the bottom of a steep drop marks the beginning of the descent into Fourth of July Canyon. Take the right fork and drop quickly into the canyon. In a few hundred yards, the route crosses the Big Ditch for the last time, but the steep road requires all the rider's attention. To understand how the ditch had to contour the topography to reach its goal, consider this: to this point by road from the last crossing of the ditch it is a half-mile; the ditch meandered over three miles.

Continue the short and steep drop through Fourth of July Canyon. About one mile from the head of the canyon, reach the paved NM 538. Turn right and continue three miles back to the car park.

Background

For centuries the secluded Moreno Valley was home to native wildlife and wandering Jicarilla Apaches and Ute Indians. In the summer of 1866, a casual discovery by a group of Ute hunters ended the Moreno Valley's isolation. While stalking game on the slopes of Mount Baldy, the hunters found a few fragments of blue-green rock, which they took back to the Cimarron Agency. Soldiers from Fort Union saw the rock and hired one of the hunters to take them to the mountain to find the source of the copper ore. They quickly located the copper-rich rock and staked a claim, but they also discovered gold in the gravels of Willow Creek. With copper forgotten and a vow of silence, the men returned to Fort Union to await spring. Once there, however, they could not keep their secret, and the gold rush to the Moreno Valley was on.

When the discoverers returned to their workings in spring, the valley was already crowded. The Mount Baldy Mining District was organized in May 1867. Throughout the summer, the New Mexico press hummed with stories of miners hitting fifteen cents per pan, which certainly sounded like it beat working for a living. By fall, a town had appeared near the richest placers. By its first winter, Elizabethtown—E'Town for short—had twenty buildings, five stores, several saloons, and a great deal of unfinished construction. One hundred thousand dollars of gold was taken from the surrounding streams during the first summer, and the future of the Moreno Valley residents seemed bright.

Although the gravels of the Moreno Valley were rich with gold, there was a serious drawback to producing a profitable placer mine. In winter, the snows of the high valley were too deep to allow much mining activity; in summer, the streams draining from the peaks often dried up before they reached the gold-bearing gravels. Gold could be washed from the gravels only during a few months of the year.

Lucien Maxwell, owner of the Maxwell Land Grant, where the mining took place, recognized the potential for a lucrative money-making scheme. If he could bring water to the mines in the Moreno Valley, he could charge miners both for the use of his land and for using the water they needed to continue mining. Maxwell and several other investors organized the Moreno Water and Mining Company, whose chartered purpose was to supply water year-round to miners in the gulches surrounding Elizabethtown.

Maxwell hired a civil engineer to design a solution to the water problem. Captain Nicholas Davis, a Civil War veteran, proposed a system of flumes and canals to bring water to the Moreno Valley. Davis' plan called for drawing water from over the mountains at the head of the Red River. Moreno Valley miners were jubilant over the plans and predicted the project would provide enough water for thousands of men for at least twenty years.

Although it is only eleven miles from the head of the Red River to Elizabethtown, the Moreno Valley Canal, which soon was generally known as the Big Ditch, had to contour around hills and canyons for a distance of forty miles before reaching the mines. Work began in May 1868, and there was much to be done. Huge trees for flumes were located, cut and hauled. Long sections of canal were dug. Aqueducts were built to span some deeper canyons; one half-mile section of flume had to be raised seventy-nine feet off the ground to cross the divide between the two watersheds. In summer, desperate miners who could not wash gravels for lack of water joined the ditch construction crews, and soon over four hundred men were on the job. Even with the additional labor force, the ditch was still nine miles short of completion when winter forced the crews to halt. Work started again early in the spring of 1869, and the construction and repairs were completed in early July.

The plans for the ditch called for the delivery of six thousand gallons of water per hour to Humbug Gulch. Less than one thousand gallons per hour ever made it, hardly enough to support a valley full of miners. Unreliable flows at the source, leakage, breaks, and evaporation took too much water from the system. To increase the flow, flumes were added from other drainages, and small reservoirs were built at the headwaters of the Red River. After an investment of two years and over two hundred thousand dollars, and the construction of one of the great engineering feats

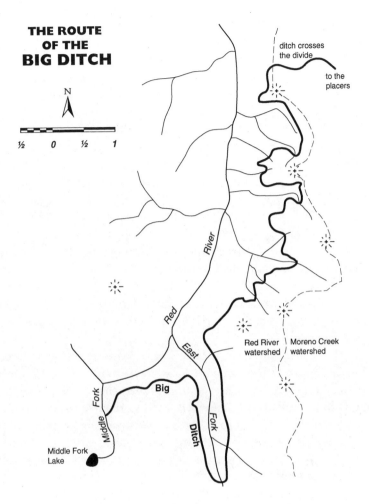

THE ROUTE
OF THE
BIG DITCH

N

½   0   ½   1

ditch crosses
the divide

to the
placers

River

Red

East

Red River   Moreno Creek
watershed / watershed

Big

Fork

Middle

Fork

Ditch

Middle Fork
Lake

in nineteenth-century New Mexico, the Big Ditch could never turn a profit.

A look at a map will show the magnitude of the task it took to create the Big Ditch. The original flume drew its water from the Middle Fork of the Red River at ten thousand feet, below Middle Fork Lake. From there, the channel winds around the contours of the steep mountainsides, detouring two miles up and back down the valley of the East Fork of the Red, dropping about twenty feet per mile along the way. The Ditch continues its incredibly convoluted course to a small saddle (at 9,850 feet) just south of Red River Pass. From here, it passes over the divide and begins a relatively easy descent into the Moreno Valley.

Through a succession of owners, some form of the Big Ditch was in operation for many years, but it never fulfilled its promise of permanence to E'Town. By 1870, the placers were empty, and most of the high grade ores were gone; the town was almost deserted by 1875. Coming to life again briefly around 1900, Elizabethtown died its final death in 1931.

Like the Big Ditch, the road to Red River Pass was another early engineering feat. At the turn of the century, when the population of Red River was only 150, the lone route into town was an old wagon road coming over from Elizabethtown; supplies were hauled by rail to Ute Park, then freighted by wagon to the Moreno Valley and over the steep mountain road. In 1914, the United States Forest Service decided to open up recreational possibilities in the Red River Valley by building a road into the town that would accommodate automobile travel. The Forest Service survey party was charged with the task of making a road with a southern exposure and with maximum grades of less than 7 percent. During the summer of 1914, the crew laid out the road's six switchbacks.

Construction began in June 1915. Beam plows were used to loosen dirt and rocks, and fresno scrapers pulled by teams of two to six horses moved material and graded the surface. Dynamite and chains pulled by horses were used to remove rocks and trees. Maneuvering teams of four horses on a steep hillside required the most skillful operators. Often the slope was so steep that much of the work had to be done with pick and shovel. By late August, the grade was only half-complete. After the winter layover, work resumed in June 1916 and was completed two months later. The finished road was twelve feet wide, paralleled by a two-foot ditch for drainage, with wooden culverts, and many turnouts for passing on the narrow roadway. The road climbed one thousand feet in four miles, reaching the pass at 9,852 feet. Red River Pass Road was used as the sole east entrance to Red River until 1966, a testament to the skills of the engineer and crew who built the road.

The Hairpin Turns of the Road on Red River Hill, ca. 1935.
(Photograph from the Duffey Collection, Courtesy, New Mexico
State Records Center and Archives, Santa Fe, No. 4369.)

Further Reading

Balcomb, Kenneth. *The Red River Hill.* Albuquerque: Albuquerque Historical Society, 1981.

Pearson, Jim Berry. *The Red River–Twining Area: A New Mexico Mining Story.* Albuquerque: University of New Mexico Press, 1986.

Chapter 7
Pioneer Canyon
■■■■■■■■■■■■■■■■■■■■■■■■

Location: south of Red River, Sangre de Cristo
    Mountains, Carson National Forest
Distance: 8 miles
Elevation: 8,600 to 10,200 feet
Elevation Change: 1,600 feet
Skill Level: difficult
Seasons: mid-June to mid-October
Ride Surface: dirt and gravel roads
Interesting Features: mines, mine dumps, mining
    cabins, mill ruins, quiet canyon with running
    water
Maps: Carson National Forest, USGS Red River 7.5-
    minute quadrangle

Access
●●●●●●●●●●●●●●●●●●●

About one-quarter mile from the west end of Main Street
in the town of Red River, turn south onto Pioneer Road. Cross the
Red River and drive 0.2 miles toward the ski area. Park in the
large lot near the ski area and the Arrowhead Lodge.

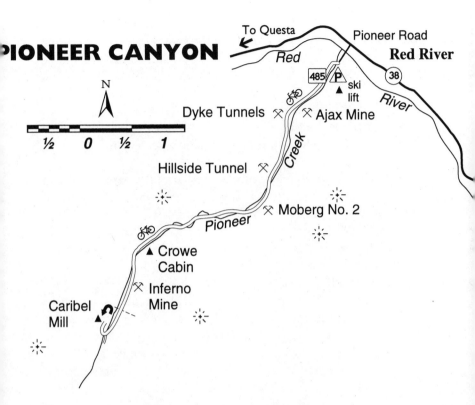

PIONEER CANYON

To Questa

Pioneer Road

Red River

Red River

485   P   ski lift

Dyke Tunnels   Ajax Mine

N

½   0   ½   1

Creek

Hillside Tunnel

Moberg No. 2

Pioneer

Crowe Cabin

Inferno Mine

Caribel Mill

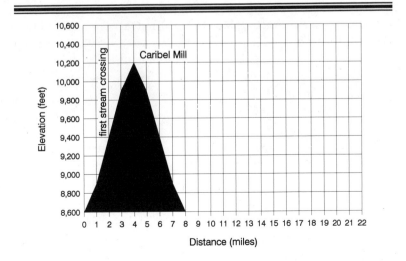

Ride Description

The ride up Pioneer Canyon is a perfect mountain bike exploration. There is much to see in the short eight miles of riding from Red River to the Caribel Mill and back, so riders should be prepared to spend at least half a day in the canyon. The route is a constant climb, but there are enough scenic stops to keep riders rested. To avoid the many jeep tours that head up the canyon, do this ride early in the day. Remember that mine tunnels and dumps are potentially dangerous; and use caution when exploring around the old prospects in the canyon.

Head toward the northwest corner of the parking lot and cross the bridge over Pioneer Creek just in front of the office of the Arrowhead Lodge. Immediately turn left onto FR 485 and climb a short hill. For more details about Pioneer Canyon, pick up the excellent Forest Service brochure at the sign announcing the entrance to Pioneer Canyon Historic Area.

Ride FR 485 past the ski lift and ski area maintenance yards. During the first mile, a few small mines are visible across the stream, recognizable as piles of orange rocks a few yards up the slope. The most important of these is the Ajax Mine, located about a half-mile up the canyon. Just short of a mile up the canyon, at stop number two on the Forest Service trail, park and explore the mine tunnels just above road level and on the cliffs above. These are the Dyke Tunnels, gold mines first worked in 1917. The timbers at the entrance to the lower tunnel and in the upper tunnels were part of a reworking of the mine in 1948.

Look for more mine dumps and tunnels in the next half mile. About 1.5 miles up the canyon, just before the first stream crossing, park and walk up a steep side road (at trail marker number six) to visit a well-preserved miner's cabin, with interesting features inside. The cabin and adjacent mine were the property of Lily Smith, who operated at least a half-dozen mines in lower Pioneer Canyon in the 1920s.

Continue up the road, making the first wet crossing of Pioneer Creek. The next stop (number nine) is at a large cleared area on the left. Here are the remains of a cabin, outhouse, and storage shed, all built by Harry Moberg and his family. Behind the ruins, blue and green copper minerals and white chunks of the mineral calcite can be found on the mine dumps. On top of the larger dump is the mine tunnel and, above it, a large collapse

The Lily Smith Cabin in Pioneer Canyon

trench—a potent reminder of why mining tunnels are dangerous places.

The road now steepens as it continues the long climb. About one mile and three stream crossings beyond the Moberg place, explore a large collapsed structure on the right side of the road (at number thirteen). This property was owned by Billy Anderson, who worked his tunnels in the 1920s. The most interesting feature is the dynamite shed leaning into the hillside behind the cabin ruins. A short distance up the road on the left is a well-preserved cabin, with an attached work shed, built by George Crowe in the 1920s.

Above the Crowe cabin, the stream joins the road for about fifty yards. Continue on the road to the left of the stream and begin a steep climb. The road levels out for a short distance at the Inferno Mine where the tunnel, a recently constructed cabin, and a railbed connecting the mine and the dump are found.

Above the Inferno is another steep, rocky climb. As the road levels out, ride to a gate. This marks the boundary of the private land surrounding the Caribel workings. If the gate is closed or posted, this is the turnaround point. If the gate is open and not posted "No Trespassing," continue up the road. Beyond the gate, the road forks. Turn right and immediately come to cabin ruins and the huge wood and concrete remains of the Caribel Mill. When exploring the extensive ruins, treat them with respect to ensure access in the future: parts of the mill seem held together by spider webs.

After touring the Caribel Mill, return to Red River by the same route. On the way, use caution on the many steep downhill sections of the road.

Background

A common thread linking the fates of those who invested their money and lives in the mines of the Red River area is disappointment. The mountains and canyons surrounding the Red River Valley were worked almost entirely by small-scale operators seeking the one find that would make them rich. No matter where they dug, they found tantalizing color, but the ores were almost never rich enough to pay the high costs of transporting them out of the remote valley to processing plants in Denver or beyond.

Take the example of Harry W. Moberg. Moberg arrived in Pioneer Canyon in the early 1900s and established eight claims on which he staked his life. Each claim showed good color, and hopes were high that at least one of them would make the family fortune. On a small flat above Pioneer Creek, he and his family built a cabin, storage sheds, and a spring house. Moberg developed all eight of his claims, investing the most time on Number Two, located just behind his cabin, where he tunneled into the mountain about three thousand feet. Several tons of ore were shipped to Colorado but failed to produce enough profit to call for more shipments. After thirty years in the canyon, Moberg died of pneumonia in 1935, with no material gain to show for his many years of hard work.

The upper Red River saw its first prospectors in the spring of 1871 as miners from Elizabethtown and Taos drifted in over the high passes in search of gold. Although groups worked the valley throughout the 1870s, the first strike was made in 1879 when a rich copper deposit was located near the present town of Red River. In what would become a familiar story, after piling ore and constructing a mill, the high cost of transportation forced the miners to abandon their project.

The mining history of Pioneer Canyon begins during this first phase of Red River history when the Pioneer Mining Company opened the district in July of 1883. The company worked three major mines: the Hannibal, the De Soto, and the Hep. Others followed the news and began digging in the canyon. A small collection of tents near the mouth of the canyon formed the first community in the Red River Valley. The Pioneer Company worked in the canyon for two years but failed to locate a rich ore.

Scattered small-time operations continued in Red River area throughout the 1880s, but none could turn a profit. The valley was empty when the Mallette brothers arrived in 1892 and established a homestead near the present town. Shortly afterward, gold strikes in La Belle brought miners back to Red River, and soon there were enough people in the valley to lay out a town site.

Besides farming, the Mallette brothers did some prospecting. In 1896, they discovered a rich ore at their Ajax claim in Pioneer Canyon. Although little mining was done at the Ajax, the find brought a new wave of exploration into the canyon. Many mines were opened in the next few years, enough to interest the Red River Mining Company in building what the town needed most: a smelter. The plant was built in 1897, but, incredibly, no one could properly operate the mill to extract metal from the tricky Red River ores. The plant was soon shut down.

Nothing could deter the efforts of the Red River supporters who always held faith that a rich strike and prosperity for the town were just around the corner. In the summer of 1898, hopeful miners stopped their tunneling and built the road up Pioneer Canyon. Rumors that another mill would be built again sent miners scurrying up the new road to stockpile ore. The new June Bug Mill was built, but again results were disappointing, triggering an exodus from the canyon. For a dozen years, Pioneer Canyon was left to hardy souls like Harry Moberg and Lily Smith.

Not all mining ventures in the Red River area were unsuccessful. About four miles up Pioneer Canyon is the Caribel Mine. In the summer of 1913, the Caribel was the busiest place in the Red River area. Rich gold and silver ore had prompted the Caribel Mining and Milling Company to construct a small mill at the site. Three shifts a day worked on the main tunnel, and the mill was producing as much as one thousand dollars of gold per day, with small amounts of silver adding to the profits. Although flooding in the tunnels slowed operations for a few months each summer, the Caribel remained an active, moneymaking mine through 1916.

Sensing a chance for greater profits, the company raised the capital to build a larger mill at the site. In 1917, the new cyanide operation began. For a small canyon, the water-powered Caribel Mill was a huge operation. Using a five-stamp crusher, the new mill was able to process twenty-five tons of ore per day. Near the mill, the company built bunkhouses, an assay office, a blacksmith shop, and a compress shed. Two years of digging failed to raise the profits, and in 1919 the mine was closed. Attemps to revive the opertion were made throughout the next fifteen years,but the Caribel was finished, closing permanently in the early 1930s.

Further Reading

Hubley, Pat, Jonathan Dean, and Nancy Zoellmer. *Pioneer Canyon Trail: Mining History of Red River.* United States Forest Service Pamphlet, Carson National Forest, n.d.

Pearson, Jim Berry. *The Red River–Twining Area: A New Mexico Mining Story.* Albuquerque: University of New Mexico Press, 1986.

Chapter 8
Garcia Homestead
■■■■■■■■■■■■■■■■■■■■■■■■■■■■

Location: north of Los Alamos, Jemez Mountains, Santa Fe National Forest

Distance: 24 miles

Elevation: 6,400 to 7,100 feet

Elevation Change: 1,900 feet

Skill Level: moderate

Seasons: muddy from December to March, and after recent summer rains, best during spring and fall

Ride Surface: dirt and gravel roads

Interesting Features: pumice mines, homestead ruins, Anasazi cliff dwellings

Maps: Santa Fe National Forest, USGS Puye and Guaje Mountain 7.5-minute quadrangles

Access
●●●●●●●●●●●●●●●●●●●

From Santa Fe, go north on US 84/285 to Pojoaque, then turn left on NM 502 toward Los Alamos. Continue ten miles to a water tank on the right, 0.8 miles past the intersection with NM 30. Turn right onto a gravel road (FR 57) that travels on San Ildefonso Pueblo land. Continue up this well-maintained road 3.5 miles and bear right onto FR 442 at a Y-intersection. After one mile on FR 442, park at the junction with FR 416 at the bottom of a steep hill climbing the side of a mesa.

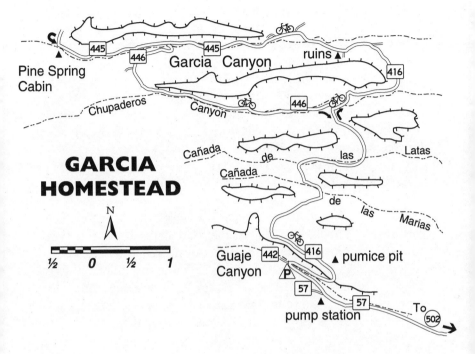

**GARCIA
HOMESTEAD**

N

½   0   ½   1

Pine Spring Cabin

445

446

445

Garcia Canyon

ruins

416

Chupaderos Canyon

446

Cañada

de

las

Latas

Cañada

de

las

Marias

Guaje Canyon

442

416

pumice pit

P

57

57

To 502

pump station

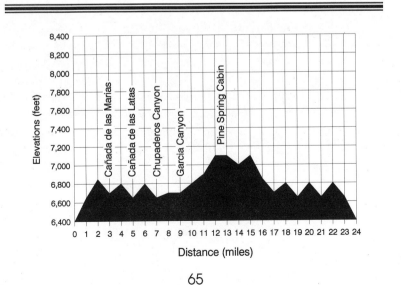

Ride Description

■ ■ ■ ■ ■ ■ ■ ■ ■ ■ ■ ■ ■

Begin by climbing the steep shelf road, FR 416. At the top of the mesa ride through a working pumice mine; use caution if construction equipment is present. It is worth stopping at the pit to study the walls of bedded pumice. The source of the pumice is the violent eruptions of the Jemez Volcano, the remnants of which make up the western skyline.

Continue riding on FR 416 past an overlook into Guaje Canyon. The road winds along a mesa top studded with juniper and piñon pine before dropping into the first of four canyons to be crossed, Cañada de las Marias.

From the bottom of Cañada de las Marias, the road climbs a short but steep saddle to cross into Cañada de las Latas (Spanish for tin plates or bores). The drop into this canyon is paralleled by a long mesa composed of orange Bandelier tuff. After climbing out of the Cañada de las Latas, the road again drops, this time into Chupaderos Canyon. (The origin of the name is unclear, but it derives from the Spanish for either sinkhole or cattle tick.) Pass the intersection with FR 446, the return leg of this loop, coming in from the left. FR 416 rounds the end of a long mesa, goes through a gate, then drops into Garcia Canyon, passing abandoned pumice mines on the way.

At an unmarked T-intersection, turn left. Ride a half mile beyond the intersection, then watch for a well-worn dirt track that goes left just after you rise out of a small gully. Turn left onto the track and ride one hundred yards from the road to one of the ruins of the Garcia homestead. Explore the dugout, taking care not to disturb anything.

Return to FR 416 and continue west. To the left, amidst fields of sage and other low-growing plants are the remains of the Garcia homestead croplands. At the next T-intersection, turn left onto FR 445, which continues to follow Garcia Canyon. Anasazi cliff rooms are located along the south face of the mesas to the west; a short side road leads to a closer view of these ruins. South of the road are more homestead buildings, but these remain on private land and are fenced off. Respect the landowners and keep out.

Continue up Garcia Canyon to the intersection with FR 446. Take the right fork for a four-mile side trip to Pine Springs and a pleasant lunch spot; take the left fork, FR 446, to continue the loop. FR 446 climbs a low saddle before dropping into

Chupaderos Canyon. The next three miles are shady and down-hill. Return to FR 416, turn right, and backtrack the last five miles through Cañada de las Latas and Cañada de las Marias to the car park.

Background

Volcanic features dominate this pleasant ride across three mesas and into steep-walled canyons cut into the soft rocks of the Pajarito Plateau. The plateau makes up the flanks of the Jemez Mountains, the remnants of a lofty volcano whose final eruptions one million years ago produced the dominant features of the landscape.

The Jemez Volcano was built slowly during fifteen million years of activity, but it ended its active life with a series of explosive eruptions that blew several thousand feet off the top of the mountain, collapsed the summit, and formed the deep, crater-like caldera in the center of the Jemez Mountains today. The initial stage of these final explosions covered much of what would be the Pajarito Plateau with massive quantities of pumice. Pumice is lightweight volcanic glass riddled with gas pockets. As the pumice fell from the sky, it landed in beds that are often sorted into fine and coarse-grained layers. The eastern plateau is dotted with a half-dozen pumice mines, and bedding is found in the walls of the pits.

Later stages of the final eruptions of the Jemez Volcano hurled huge quantities of volcanic ash down the mountainsides—picture the gray-blue cauliflower clouds that the eruption of Mt. St. Helens made famous. As the hot ash settled on the flanks of the volcano, it fused, cooling slowly to form a soft rock known as Bandelier tuff. The long, orange cliffs characteristic of the Pajarito Plateau are composed of this fused volcanic ash.

A million years of erosion have cut deeply into the soft tuff of the Pajarito Plateau, creating deep, secluded valleys. The broad tablelands dotted with juniper and piñon pine first attracted the Anasazi and later Hispano ranchers. Traditional use of the Pajarito Plateau for farming and ranching had a long history, and some homesteads date back to the nineteenth century. In 1906, most of the plateau was opened to homesteading, and by 1910 more than thirty homesteads were established on the mesas.

The Garcia family took out patents on lands in the eastern foothills of the Jemez Mountains beginning in 1892. Their first homestead was in the canyon that acquired the family name. Juan

Luis Garcia acquired 160 acres, built cabins for his family, and cleared by hand extensive fields on the flat benches above the canyon bottom to raise crops. Over the next fifty years, Garcia's sons took out patents on surrounding lands and in adjacent canyons. The family complex grew to cover almost two miles of the canyon and included fields, barns, cabins, springs, and—for a time—a sawmill.

The Garcias owned a small farm south of Española that served as their primary and winter residence; use of the homestead was strictly seasonal. Juan Luis would come up the rough road in Santa Clara Canyon to his homestead in late March to plant wheat, plowing fields with crude tools and a horse. Later, as the school year permitted, his sons and daughters would join him to plant beans, potatoes, and corn. This was dry farming with no irrigation. Crop success was dependent on the summer rains, and there were some lean years when the crops failed. Nonetheless, beans were a good cash crop. Harvested in the fall, the beans were dried and sold in the communities of northern New Mexico throughout the winter. Additional cash was earned by picking piñon nuts and, when the sawmill was operating, from selling lumber and vigas for new home construction.

Because the use of the homestead was seasonal, the Garcias had no need to build an elaborate home in the canyon. Most structures were for farm animals and only a few small dwellings were ever needed. The tuff-block cabin found along the road in Garcia Canyon remains in good condition after almost seventy-five years. Dug into the side of a gully and constructed with materials from the surrounding land, the structure blends perfectly with the landscape. The walls are composed of tuff blocks chinked with adobe; the roof is mud and sod, supported with ponderosa pine beams. Inside are the remains of crude plank furniture, preserved by the dry New Mexican air.

The canyon remained in the Garcia family until 1942 when the lands were condemned by the U. S. Government for the Manhattan Project. Disputes over land ownership began after the war, and today part of the homestead has been returned to private hands.

Further Reading

Hoard, Dorothy. *Los Alamos Outdoors*. Los Alamos, New Mexico: Los Alamos Historical Society, 1981.

Kudo, A. M. "Outline of the Geology of the Jemez Mountains Volcanic Field." In *New Mexico Geological Society Guidebook, 25th Field Conference*. Socorro: New Mexico Geological Society, 1974.

Rothman, Hal. *On Rims and Ridges: The Los Alamos Area Since 1880*. Lincoln: University of Nebraska Press, 1992.

Chapter 9
Cebolla Canyon

■■■■■■■■■■■■■■■■■■■■■■■■■■

Location: southeast of Grants, El Malpais
    Conservation Area
Distance: 23 miles
Elevation: 7,300 to 7,500 feet
Elevation Change: 400 feet
Skill Level: easy
Seasons: May through October
Ride Surface: dirt roads
Interesting Features: wilderness canyon, homestead
    ruins, sawmill ruins, solitude
Maps: El Malpais Recreation Guide Map, USGS
    Cebollita Peak and Sand Canyon 7.5-minute
    quadrangles

Access

● ● ● ● ● ● ● ● ● ● ● ● ● ● ● ● ● ●

From Grants, take I-40 east for four miles to exit 89. From Albuquerque, exit 89 is about sixty-five miles west. Go south on NM 117 about twenty-six miles, passing the El Malpais Ranger Station and La Ventana Arch. About 8.5 miles past the turnoff to La Ventana, look for a large metal gate and an unmarked dirt road (Cebolla Canyon Road) on the east side of NM 117. Go through the gate (be certain to close it), pass a windmill on the left, and drive in about a mile. Park off the road at any convenient place.

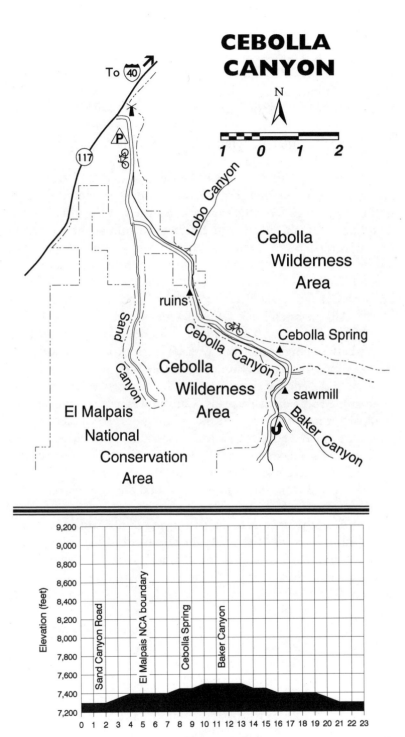

CEBOLLA CANYON

To (40)

N

1 0 1 2

Lobo Canyon

(117)

P

Cebolla
Wilderness
Area

ruins

Cebolla Canyon

Cebolla Spring

Sand Canyon

Cebolla
Wilderness
Area

sawmill

Baker Canyon

El Malpais
National
Conservation
Area

Ride Description

━━ ━━ ━━ ━━ ━━ ━━ ━━ ━━ ━━ ━━

The Cebolla Canyon Road cuts the Cebolla Wilderness Area in half, providing mountain bike riders the unique opportunity of pedaling through, while not officially in, a wilderness. Although neither remote nor difficult to access, Cebolla Canyon receives few visitors, increasing the feeling of a wilderness experience. Remember that mountain bikes are prohibited in the wilderness, and stay on the main road.

Begin by riding south on the Cebolla Canyon Road. The first six miles of this route cross private land, so stay on the road. About three miles from the car park, bear left at the intersection with Sand Canyon Road, and continue to follow the valley of Cebolla Creek. Shortly after this turn, cross a deep arroyo. The flat ride through open pastures and between the high mesas is fast and exhilarating. About five miles from the start, enjoy the views up Lobo Canyon to the left.

After passing Lobo Canyon, cross the El Malpais Conservation Area boundary. The road now enters Cebolla Canyon and passes between high sandstone walls. The arroyo in the middle of the canyon is deeply cut, an unmistakable sign of past overgrazing. Along the edge of the arroyo for the next two miles are scattered stone ruins of homesteads. Cans and ranch equipment are flung about near the ruins. At the crossing of the Cebolla Creek, about 1.5 miles above the El Malpais boundary, look left for a large slab of sandstone with wonderful ripple marks, and search the sandstone layers for abundant fossils. Other ruins in this area can be spotted from the road, but, as they are in the wilderness area, must be reached on foot.

After the stream crossing, the route climbs and drops from a small ridge. Beyond is a flat, soggy pasture, often filled with what can best be described as "quickmud." Two miles beyond the crossing are Cebolla Spring and more ruins, this time wooden frame shelters. These relics are on private land, so view them from the road. Cross a small arroyo and bear right (if indeed the side road to the left can be seen). As the road swings south, enjoy the broad flats as four or five canyons join in a small area.

About a mile from the spring, at the base of the left canyon wall, look for the waste from an old sawmill. Just beyond is a fork in the road. This is a good turnaround point. Alternatively, riders can take the left fork and climb the ridge for a long loop along Baker Canyon or continue up the Cebolla Valley by taking the right fork. When finished, turn around and retrace the route through the Cebolla Canyon to the car park.

Background

In terms of a human lifetime, changes to the landscape usually come slowly. Indeed, with the exceptions of the instantaneous changes brought by earthquakes and volcanoes, most geologic transformations evolve over millions of years. Like Rome, the Sandia, Jemez, Sangre de Cristo, and other mountain ranges in New Mexico were not built in a day, or even over thousands of years.

In contrast, when humans impact the environment, changes to the landscape can occur rapidly. In the southwest, the appearance of much of the land has been radically altered over the past one hundred years. The most significant differences are along watercourses. In the past, permanent water flowed in many streams now often dry, for example the Rio Puerco, Chaco Wash, and Cebolla Creek. Travellers to New Mexico in the mid-1800s described the valleys of such rivers as lush with vegetation, oases in the desert. Today, these floodplains are not only dry much of the year, but are dissected by deeply entrenched arroyos, steep-walled miniature canyons cut to surprising depth in just one hundred years.

It is no accident that the most recent episode of arroyo cutting in the southwest began in the late 1880s, just after the arrival of the railroads. With the railroads came the opportunity to transport, at low cost, cattle raised in New Mexico to markets in the mid-West and East. The once empty rangelands of New Mexico exploded with activity. From 1880 to 1890, the number of cattle in the state increased tenfold; the number of sheep also saw a dramatic increase. Much of the new grazing centered on the well-watered valleys and the surrounding acres of untouched rangeland.

Grazing animals can severely impact the land. Most damaging is trampling of soil. Pounding hooves compact the upper layer of earth and make it difficult for water to infiltrate. Rather than seeping into the ground, rainwater ponds and flows on the surface, channeled along miles of stock-created trails. Feeding and trampling also take a severe toll on vegetation, stripping the land of its native grasses and replacing them with less dense, less desirable cover. Compaction of soil and changes in vegetation combine to decrease the land's ability to absorb water, leading to a dramatic increase in runoff.

Increased runoff directly led to the formation of arroyos. Where once spring and summer floods lost energy by spreading over broad floodplains, an increased volume of water runoff and new channels cut from stock trails began the downcutting. Once started, the process of arroyo cutting fed on itself by gathering increasing amounts of water at ever higher velocities. The depth of larger arroyos is testament enough to the power of the process.

By 1890, arroyos were common in the southwest. Thirty years later, the effects of arroyo cutting were felt throughout the agricultural community. Rather than flowing on the floor of the valleys, entrenched streams flowed ten to thirty feet below the level of the surrounding fields. Without extensive and costly improvements, the water within the streams was unavailable for irrigation—if there was flowing water at all. Disruption of the hydrologic cycle, subsiding water tables, and rapid runoff of precipitation all led to a new flow regime in the streams. The arroyos were commonly dry for most of the year. However, during spring or after heavy summer thunderstorms, floods of unprecedented force roared down the channels.

Homesteading in the southwest began coincidentally with the coming of the railroad and the new boom in ranching. From the mid-1880s to 1920, small-scale ranchers took up the government's offer of free acres for the price of improvements to

Homestead Ruins in Cebolla Canyon

74

the land. In well-watered valleys like Cebolla Canyon, ranches were strung out the length of the stream, and untold numbers of cattle grazed in the surrounding hills. As the environment was altered and arroyo cutting increased, the homesteaders found they could not irrigate their fields, and that their water supply was unreliable. The rangelands became increasingly poor in quality, leaving little hope to eke out even a meager existence. By 1935, the homesteads of Cebolla Canyon, and of most of the rest of the southwest, were abandoned.

Further Reading

DuBuys, William. *Enchantment and Exploitation.* Albuquerque: University of New Mexico Press, 1988.

Chapter 10
Amoxiumqua
■■■■■■■■■■■■■■■■■■■

Location: Jemez Mountains, Santa Fe National
   Forest
Distance: 22 miles
Elevation: 7,700 to 8,600 feet
Elevation Change: 1,200 feet
Skill Level: moderate
Seasons: May to June, September to late October
Ride Surface: gravel roads and double track, with
   stretches of soft sand
Interesting Features: overlook of Cañon de San
   Diego and Jemez Springs, ruins of a logging
   camp, large Anasazi ruin
Maps: Santa Fe National Forest, USGS Jemez Springs
   7.5-minute quadrangle

Access
● ● ● ● ● ● ● ● ● ● ● ● ● ● ● ● ● ●

   Take NM 4 north from San Ysidro, or west from Los
Alamos, to the village of La Cueva in the heart of the Jemez Mountains. From La Cueva, drive north toward Cuba on NM 126 for
three miles to FR 376. Turn left on this well-maintained gravel
road and go one mile to FR 604. Turn left onto FR 604 and park
in the meadow at the bottom of the hill.

AMOXIUMQUA

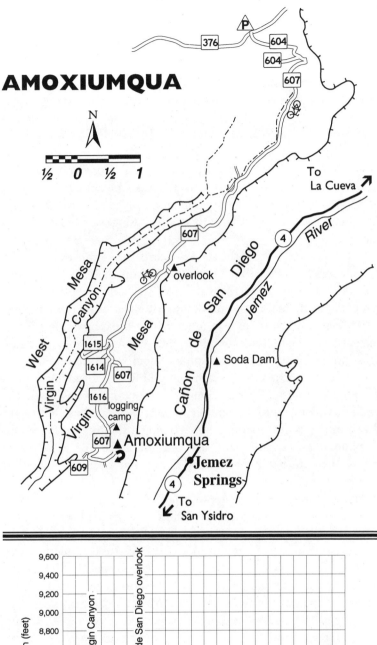

N

½ 0 ½ 1

376

604
604

607

P

To
La Cueva

607

overlook

West   Mesa   Canyon

Virgin

Mesa

1615
1614
607
1616
logging
camp

609
607

Amoxiumqua

Cañon   de   San   Diego   Jemez   River

4

Soda Dam

Jemez
Springs

4

To
San Ysidro

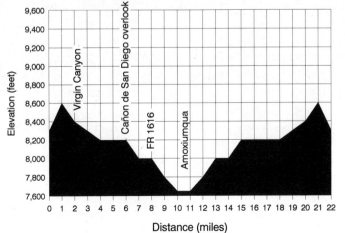

Ride Description

▬ ▬ ▬ ▬ ▬ ▬ ▬ ▬ ▬ ▬ ▬ ▬ ▬ ▬

Begin riding on FR 604, immediately climbing a long hill to the top of the mesa. A little more than a mile from the start, turn left onto FR 607. Ride east, then south on FR 607. Soon the road passes through an old burn area before dropping down an aspen-shaded hillside. The road to the left at a minor junction about 1.5 miles from the start leads to an interesting overlook down Wildcat Canyon. The next 1.5 miles is through a narrow meadow that is part of the uppermost drainage of Virgin Canyon. An old corral is a reminder of this valley's long use for cattle grazing.

Four miles from the start is a three-way intersection. Take the left fork, still FR 607, climbing up a short but rocky hill. After the trail levels out, ride through short stretches of soft tuff sand (volcanic ash). Ignore the numerous side routes to the left until two miles past the three-way junction. At this point, the edge of the mesa is in sight; look for a road that leads to the edge, and ride one hundred yards to the overlook and enjoy the view.

From the overlook, continue on FR 607 through the ponderosa pine forest. One-and-a-half miles beyond the overlook, FR 1615 provides a half-mile side trip to West Mesa and a view straight down into Virgin Canyon. After crossing a shallow drainage and climbing the other side, turn right onto FR 1616. (FR 607 continues to the ruin but is badly eroded and has been barricaded in many places with dirt berms.) Follow FR 1616 for a little more than a mile until it again meets FR 607. On the hillside above this junction are the remains of the cabins of a 1920s logging camp, complete with rusting stoves and piles of tin cans.

Continue another half-mile on FR 607 to the junction with FR 609. Take a hard left and in a quarter-mile another left to the ruins of Amoxiumqua. The site is huge—an open structure consisting of four connected rectangles. Most of the tuff-block masonry walls are covered with grasses and overgrown, but the outline of the continpueblo and the kiva depressions are clearly visible. Thousands of pot shards litter the ground. (Remember all artifacts are protected by the Antiquities Act: leave the pottery where it is found!) Explore the perimeter of the ruin, and savor the same expansive view the Pueblos enjoyed hundreds of years ago. Return to the car park by the same route.

Background

— — — — — — — — — —

    Amoxiumqua—"anthill place"—is a large Pueblo ruin located on the edge of Cañon de San Diego. The ruin, about six hundred by one thousand feet, is twice the size of the better-known Tyuonyi in Frijoles Canyon at Bandelier National Monument. The village holds three plazas on three different levels, and much of the pueblo was probably two or three stories high. Limited excavation carried out from 1910 to 1914 by the Bureau of American Ethnology and the Royal Ontario Museum left archaeologists with little knowledge of Amoxiumqua's history. However, the study revealed the site was occupied from around 1300 to 1500 and then abandoned. The pueblo was again occupied when the Spanish arrived in the area in the late sixteenth century; the inhabitants aban-

Workers during the Excavation of Amoxiumqua, October 1912. (Photograph by Wesley Bradfield, Courtesy, Museum of New Mexico, Santa Fe, Negative No. 150148.)

doned the town a second time during the seventeenth century, probably moving to the modern pueblo of Jemez in the canyon below.

    On the way to Amoxiumqua, the view from the mesa edge into the Cañon de San Diego is spectacular. The canyon, cut by the Jemez River through soft volcanic rocks, is two thousand feet deep. The river has carved a cross section of rocks, from the red Abo sandstone, laid down before the Age of the Dinosaurs, to the orange-tan Bandelier tuff, only one million years old. The overlook is above a large group of tent rocks, conical shapes of tuff formed by the action of hot gases working their way through the ash when it was still warm. Far below, look for the Soda Dam, a large deposit of travertine left behind by cooling water from the hot springs along the river. On the far wall of the canyon, you can see an old river channel in the red rocks that was filled by volcanic ash during eruptions of the Jemez Volcano.

Further Reading

Reiter, P. *Monographs No. 5 and 6: Jemez Pueblo and Amoxiumqua Ruin.* Santa Fe: School of American Research, 1938.

PART 2

Old Roads

Chapter 11
The Camino Real I: Picuris Peak

■■■■■■■■■■■■■■■■■■■■■■■■■■

Location: south of Taos, Picuris Range, Carson National Forest
Distance: 17 miles
Elevation: 7,600 to 10,800 feet
Elevation Change: 3,200 feet
Skill Level: difficult
Seasons: snow-free from mid-June to mid-October
Ride Surface: dirt roads and double track
Interesting Features: the Camino Real, spectacular views
Maps: Carson National Forest, USGS Peñasco, Ranchos de Taos, and Taos SW 7.5-minute quadrangles

Access

●●●●●●●●●●●●●●●●●●●

From Española travel north on NM 68 about eighteen miles to NM 75. Turn right toward Dixon, continuing fifteen miles to Peñasco. At the intersection with NM 73 in Peñasco, bear left, still following NM 75 two miles to Vadito. One-quarter mile past the bridge over the Rio Pueblo, turn left onto FR 469. Drive about one hundred yards and park in a large open area on the left.

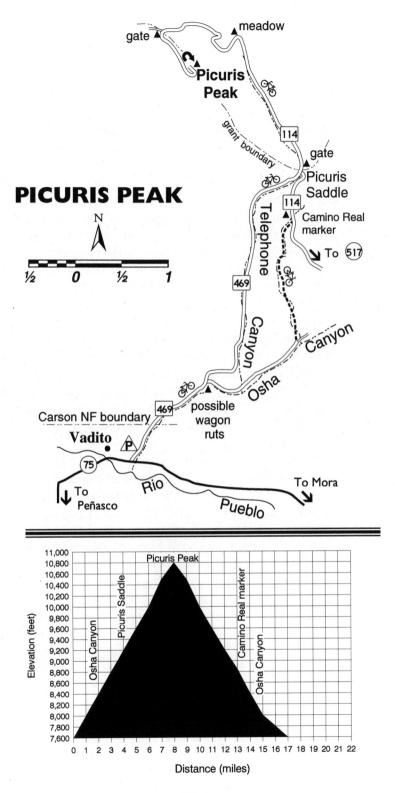

PICURIS PEAK

N

½   0   ½   1

meadow

gate

Picuris Peak

grant boundary

114

gate

Picuris Saddle

114

Camino Real marker

To 517

469

Telephone Canyon

Osha Canyon

Carson NF boundary

469

possible wagon ruts

Vadito P

75

To Peñasco

Rio Pueblo

To Mora

Picuris Peak

Osha Canyon

Picuris Saddle

Camino Real marker

Osha Canyon

Elevation (feet)

11,000
10,800
10,600
10,400
10,200
10,000
9,800
9,600
9,400
9,200
9,000
8,800
8,600
8,400
8,200
8,000
7,800
7,600

0 1 2 3 4 5 6 7 8 9 10 11 12 13 14 15 16 17 18 19 20 21 22

Distance (miles)

Ride Description

▬▬▬▬▬▬▬▬▬▬▬▬

Begin riding on FR 469 up Telephone Canyon. The route immediately begins climbing and doesn't let up until reaching Picuris Peak. In a quarter-mile, cross a cattle guard at the Carson National Forest boundary. The first four miles are characterized by alternating gentle and steep climbs, but riding the mud and gravel surface is not difficult.

About one mile from the start, the route enters a large meadow. Just inside the meadow, between the road and the stream, is a deep gully. This rut is possibly a remnant of the Camino Real, the Royal Road, worn down as the road crossed the meadow and entered Telephone Canyon. Halfway through the meadow, the road to Osha Canyon—the return route for this ride—enters from the right. Continue straight ahead on FR 469 as it climbs steeply over a ridge and then drops again to the bottom of Telephone Canyon. The canyon here is very narrow, and the road is probably directly on top of the Camino Real. Uphill, as the canyon widens slightly, the forest road climbs onto a shelf above the stream. Throughout this section look for evidence of an old route at streamside that, in the course of the next two miles, crosses and recrosses the stream many times. Wagons could not maneuver this narrow path, and traffic along this branch of the Camino Real was limited to foot travel and pack trains.

About two miles from the start, cross over Telephone Creek and continue to climb. After the next stream crossing, look for a view of a spur from Picuris Peak looming ahead. As is usually the case, the road saves its best challenge for last. The final half-mile of the road is steep and rocky as the Camino Real climbs toward the pass to Arroyo Miranda and on to Taos. Atop the pass at Picuris Saddle is a large meadow and the junction with FR 114.

From Picuris Saddle, the road to Picuris Peak is on the private Cristoval de la Serna Grant. The landowners do not object to conscientious riders traveling the route as long as they stay on the road and do not remove anything from the grant. Pass under the large gate and follow FR 114 uphill. The route is moderately steep, made more difficult by the altitude. The road follows Telephone Creek for two miles to a small meadow on a saddle. This spot is a good resting place before the steeper, final 1.5 miles to the peak, which is visible from the meadow. Next, ride several switchbacks as the road climbs a spur ridge of Picuris Peak. After the spur, the road is cut onto a shelf traversing a steep slope.

Through the trees to the right are glimpses of Taos and the Wheeler Peak area. Ride past a rocky spur road to the right, turn a corner, walk around another gate, and again enter public land. Continue the last, steep half-mile to the summit.

It is more than a matter of pride to get a bicycle to the top of the hill. Views through the trees on the way up are just teasers compared to the 360-degree spectacular panorama visible from the summit of Picuris Peak. All of northern New Mexico is spread out below as the scene encompasses the Truchas Peaks, Sandia Mountains, Black Mesa, Taos, and the gorge of the Rio Grande.

Return from the summit on FR 114, using caution on the rocky descent. At Picuris Saddle and the junction with FR 469, turn left on FR 114 and climb out of the meadow. After a short, steep drop, stop at the Camino Real marker in another small meadow. From the sign, look down the slope and locate an abandoned road that follows the stream down this canyon, which is incorrectly identified on the sign as Osha Canyon. Follow this double track downhill. Two hundred yards downstream is another marker, this one correctly placing the Camino Real in Telephone Canyon to the west. The next 1.5 miles are grassy, muddy, and rocky, with many small trees lying across the road; although it is an old jeep road, it rides like a single track. Follow the road carefully as it makes many crossings of the small stream at the bottom. When in doubt, stick close to the canyon bottom. At a small meadow 1.5 miles from the Camino Real marker, the unnamed side canyon you have been riding in joins Osha Canyon. In a few hundred yards, the route intersects a dirt double track and continues down Osha Canyon, passing the junction with Telephone Canyon. The road skirts the edge of a large meadow and in a quarter-mile meets FR 469. Turn left and descend the last mile to the car park.

Chapter 12
The Camino Real II: La Bajada Hill

■■■■■■■■■■■■■■■■■■■■■■■■■■

Location: south of Santa Fe, Santa Fe National
Forest
Distance: 12 miles
Elevation: 5,500 to 6,350 feet
Elevation Change: 900 feet
Skill Level: moderate to the top of the mesa, easy
on the mesa top
Seasons: dry periods from mid-September to mid-
May
Ride Surface: eroded old gravel road, dirt double
track
Interesting Features: the Camino Real, historic road
from Albuquerque to Santa Fe, wagon ruts,
petroglyphs
Maps: Santa Fe National Forest, USGS Tetilla Peak
7.5-minute quadrangle

Access

• • • • • • • • • • • • • • • • •

Take I-25 south from Santa Fe or north from Albuquerque to exit 264, marked for NM 16 and Cochiti Pueblo. Travel
west on NM 16 for 3.5 miles to the road to the Tetilla Peak Recreation Area and turn right. In one mile, turn right on an unmarked
gravel road that parallels the paved road. Continue on this road
for 1.5 miles, cross the bridge over the Santa Fe River, and park on
the side of the road just past the bridge.

LA BAJADA HILL

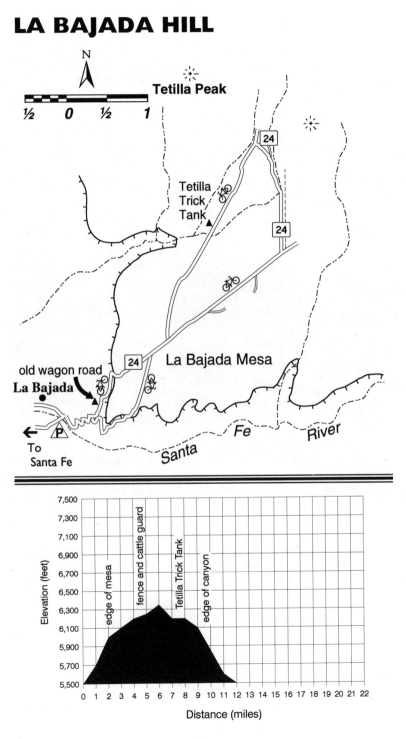

Chapter 12

Ride Description

- - - - - - - - - - - - -

From the bridge, La Bajada Hill looms ahead. The dark wall of basalt creates a formidable barrier to any traveller's progress north. Take the right fork, the unmarked FR 24, just ahead of the parking area. After crossing a small irrigation ditch, the road immediately begins climbing. The roadway is rocky and eroded, but never steep thanks to the many switchbacks that wind up the stair-like cliffs. Anasazi/Pueblo petroglyphs are found on the black basalt boulders near the first half-dozen hairpin turns. Keep a watchful eye for more petroglyphs the entire way up the hill. Continue climbing and use caution on the rutted sections of road.

Many Basalt Boulders on La Bajada Hill Are Inscribed with Petroglyphs.

About halfway up the cliff the road divides. Take the older, steeper left-hand route to the top of the cliff. On the way up, watch for basalt retaining walls built by hand around 1910. Just before the road crosses a small basalt cliff, the nineteenth-century Army wagon road is plainly visible to the left, just below the modern road. The route of this old road can be traced as it crosses a shelf and climbs steeply to the end of a switchback on the more recent road. Imagine a mule or ox-drawn wagon being hauled up the slope; the old road climbs more steeply than the newer one. Bumping over the rocks approaching the top of the hill, riders may wonder why this stretch of the Camino Real was known as The Descent and not The Ascent.

Once on top of the hill, turn and look below to locate the Camino Real as it crosses the plains to the foot of La Bajada Hill. Look for a faint rut that runs from the south to the small town of La Bajada. The nearest section of the old road runs between a powerline and the dirt entry road. The deepest ruts are on the banks of the Santa Fe River just opposite town.

Continue riding on FR 24 across La Bajada Mesa. The first half-mile of FR 24 is rocky, but riding soon becomes easier as the road stretches out on the mesa top. A half-mile from the top of the hill, watch for a road to the right, angling off to the southeast—this is the route you will later take down La Bajada Hill. While riding this straight section of road, remember that a mountain bike moves at least twice as fast as the wagons that rumbled this way during the years of Spanish trade. The road seems endless, hot, dusty and dry—and the refuge of Santa Fe would still be a day's travel away.

The mesa top is crisscrossed with confusing tracks leading in all directions. FR 24 passes a number of marked side roads leading to tanks and wells. Two-and-a-half miles from the top of La Bajada Hill, at a fence and cattle guard, turn left on FR 24 as it parallels the fence. In three-quarters of a mile the road bears left away from the fence, crosses a low ridge, and heads toward Tetilla Peak. Continue to a minor intersection. Turn left, taking the less traveled left fork, which is marked for Tetilla Trick Tank. Drop to near the bottom of a wash and turn sharply left on the road that parallels the wash. Follow the rutted double track as it heads south, back toward the edge of La Bajada Mesa. After a mile on this track, cross a shallow drainage near Tetilla Trick Tank on the right. Climb out of the drainage and continue just over one mile to FR 24. Turn right.

After a short two hundred yards on FR 24, turn left at a Y-intersection, the one noted earlier on the way up. Descend for a half-mile to the edge of the Cañada de Santa Fe; stop and enjoy the view before proceeding to learn why this section of trail became best known for the descent and not the ascent.

Pass through the gate at the top of the hill. This section of road was blasted out of the basalt in the early 1920s. Today it is badly eroded and extremely rocky. Be very cautious here; walking your bike down the first quarter-mile is highly recommended. Imagine the difficulties in bringing down the steep grade an animal-drawn wagon. Just after it is possible to begin riding again, the road skirts the very edge of the Cañada de Santa Fe. From this point the route of the Camino Real into the cañada is visible. Look for a faint depression tracking over the plain and heading directly for the river canyon. The trace of this track can be followed, crossing the small, nearby arroyos and fording the river near the mouth of the canyon.

The last portion of the descent is easy compared with the rocky first part. Pass through (and close) another gate, ride past the junction with the older road, then descend through the switchbacks to the bottom of the hill.

Background

The Camino Real is one of North America's oldest continually used roads. The route along the Rio Grande was traveled for centuries by inhabitants of the Tewa, Tiwa, Towa, Keres, and Tano pueblos as they passed from Taos to as far south as El Paso. Spanish use of the Camino Real began in 1598 when Juan Oñate led a group of five hundred colonists from Chihuahua north to settle near the confluence of the Rio Grande and the Rio Chama. From Spanish rule through the Mexican era and into the Territorial period, the Camino Real was the main route of communication from Santa Fe to points south, linking the Capitol City with Albuquerque, El Paso, Chihuahua, and the capitol of New Spain (later Mexico), Mexico City.

In its four-hundred-year history, the Camino Real has been traveled by a continuing pageant of historical figures, including virtually every person important to New Mexico's past. Colonists to farming villages, Spanish priests bringing Christianity to the Pueblos, Don Pedro de Peralta (founder of Santa Fe), Don Diego de Vargas, leaders of all the northern pueblos, Zebulon Pike, General Stephen Kearny, and Kit Carson all traveled by foot, mule, or horseback over the long, arduous route.

At first, use of the Camino Real was dominated by the supply caravans that carried goods from Spain's main colony in Mexico to the priests and settlers in and around Santa Fe. The original caravans were organized by Franciscans to supply their missions, but soon the caravans' function was broadened to include the entire colony. Eventually all transport of goods, colonists, government officials, and mail to and from New Mexico depended on the caravans.

Although law required the caravans to travel to New Mexico every three years, in reality supplies came up the Royal Road at less regular intervals. This is perhaps excusable given the knowledge that the trip to Santa Fe took about six months, as did the return to Chihuahua. By the mid-eighteenth century, the caravan had become so important that it adhered to a regular annual schedule.

The name *camino* lends too much glory to the route followed by the Spanish caravans. The road was unimproved, merely travel-packed dirt. No trail markers or accurate maps were available; ruts were the only trail signs. Early journals which describe travel along the Royal Road are replete with details of the difficulties imposed on the traveller by the landscape, weather, and river crossings.

Iron-tired, wooden wagons hauled by mules were the main method of transport during the early years along the Camino Real. Royal decree was very specific about operation of the wagon trains. Thirty-two wagons were used under the direction of four *mayordomos*. The wagons were loaded with two tons of supplies, each drawn by a team of eight mules. In addition to regular cargo, each wagon was required to carry an extensive store of emergency items such as 16 spare axles, 150 spokes, 24 spare tires, and 500 pounds of tallow for lubrication. By 1750, pack mules had replaced wagons as the main method of transport. When Conestoga wagons were brought to New Mexico by Americans traveling from Missouri over the Santa Fe Trail, many traders switched from mules to the durable "white tops."

Until the arrival of railroads in the 1880s, the Camino Real remained the most important link between northern and southern New Mexico. During the latter half of the nineteenth century, many sections of the Royal Road were improved to make travel easier for freight wagons and passenger stagecoaches. As roads were further improved to handle automobile traffic, sections of the Camino Real were paved and became part of the state and federal highway systems. Indeed, I-25 links El Paso with Albuquerque and Santa Fe by following the same basic route used by residents of the pueblos six hundred years ago.

The complaints of the Spanish explorers can still be heard loud and clear: if it isn't one thing, it's another. The problem was traveling the route from Santa Fe to Taos. On one hand was the Rio Grande, a gentle, level trail from San Ildefonso to Velarde, but the gorge beyond was too narrow and rocky for easy travel. To avoid the gorge it was necessary to journey over a bulge in the backbone of the Sangre de Cristo Mountains, the Picuris Range, a climb from 6,000 feet along the river to 9,200 feet at Picuris Saddle.

The northern stretch of the Camino Real developed as two routes. The summer route paralleled modern NM 76, the High Road to Taos, past the villages of Santa Cruz, Chimayo, and Truchas to the Rio Pueblo in the vicinity of Picuris Pueblo. This route parallels an even older one used by members of the northern pueblos for over five hundred years before the first Europeans passed through. When winter snows covered the shorter high route, travellers took the river road from Santa Cruz to Velarde, then went over the hills to Dixon, and finally proceeded roughly parallel to modern NM 75 to Picuris. From where the routes met at Picuris, there was only one way to Taos—straight over the mountains.

From the ford of the Rio Pueblo at Vadito, the Camino Real climbed steeply up Telephone Canyon to Picuris Saddle. It was, and is, a tough, steep climb of two thousand feet in four miles, and the descent down Arroyo Miranda on the other side was no easier. Once out of the mountains and onto the almost level Taos Plateau, the route led first to Ranchos de Taos and then to the town of San Fernando de Taos.

The road over Picuris Saddle was used throughout the Spanish and Mexican periods of New Mexico history, perhaps beginning in 1540 when Coronado's troops may have climbed the pass. Kit Carson and other American fur trappers, as well as part of Kearny's army of occupation, traveled this route to Taos in the 1840s. In 1854, the United States Army moved the road a few miles to the east to accommodate supply wagons traveling between Fort Burgwin south of Taos and Fort Union along the Santa Fe Trail. This second road over the Picuris Range followed the basic route of the modern NM 3.

Attacks by Utes and Apaches on the road to Taos brought further action from the Army. Within four years of the completion of the second road, the Army had plans for yet a better route. Surveyed in 1859 by Captain John Macomb, work on the third road was delayed by the Civil War and was not completed until 1874. This new route was the most difficult to build but the easiest to travel. Dug out of the rocks along the river in the Rio Grande gorge, "El Camino Militar" followed the Rio Grande from Velarde to Pilar, then climbed over the low hills to Taos, the same route followed by NM 68 today.

An impediment to any travel along the Rio Grande to and from Santa Fe is a long escarpment of basalt that makes up the southern flank of the Cerros del Rio volcanic field. The thick lavas flowed from numerous small volcanic vents along the east bank of the Rio Grande at what is now White Rock Canyon. The hard, black rock forms a cap to a small plateau southwest of Santa Fe; the plateau stands six hundred feet above the plains bordering the Rio Grande to the south. The steep pitch of the cliff face creates a natural barrier between the plains to the north and south. It was this cliff that became known to travelers along the Camino Real as La Bajada. While the name for the escarpment originated as La Majada ("a place where the sheep graze at night"), La Bajada—The Descent—was an easy corruption.

There were probably three routes leading from the Santo Domingo Pueblo past La Bajada to Santa Fe. The preferred route led to the foot of La Bajada and then followed the Santa Fe River up the Cañada de Santa Fe. Although this route traced through a rocky canyon, it followed the gentle climb of the river as it cut through the rocks of the escarpment. However, if travellers encountered high water in the canyon, not an uncommon condition, they were forced to cross the escarpment by a different route. Some travellers followed the foot of the cliff east and climbed the natural ramp from Galisteo Creek up to a low pass near where the rest area on I-25 is located today. This was a far easier route than the climb up La Bajada, but it added at least a half-day to the already overlong journey.

La Bajada Hill was used as a last resort or by travellers desperate to reach the shelter of Santa Fe. Those who chose the hill faced hours of difficult labor. Climbing six hundred feet from the Santa Fe River to the mesa top over broken, jagged rocks was no easy task for mules or ox-drawn wagons. If wagons were being used, teams would be doubled to drag the heavy loads to the top. The trip from Santa Fe, down the cliff, was even more difficult. Teamsters were forced to use ropes as brakes and needed to chock their wheels with boulders whenever they stopped.

In the late 1860s, the United States Army built the first true road up La Bajada Hill. Intended as a farm-to-market route into Santa Fe, the road soon took most of the traffic from Santa Fe to Albuquerque, including stagecoaches. As a passenger route, Lieutenant John Bourke wrote of the journey by stagecoach: "The descent was so risky that stage passengers always alighted and made their way down on foot." The Army road over La Bajada was used for forty years, and the ruts of this trail can still be found in many places on the hillside.

In 1909, the New Mexico Territorial Engineer ordered improvements to the road. The grade was relocated, a limestone gravel road bed was laid, and retaining walls of basalt were built. Although the construction of the twisting switchbacks up the hill

An Automobile Begins the Descent of La Bajada Hill in the Early 1900s. *(Photograph, Courtesy, Museum of New Mexico, Santa Fe, Negative No. 8231.)*

was meant to accommodate wagons pulled by draft animals, the new road invited use by automobiles. The old wagon ruts had gained enough dignity to become New Mexico's Road One.

Despite the improvements, auto travel up La Bajada continued to be an adventure. Washouts were frequent and under poor weather conditions a trip from Albuquerque to Santa Fe would take eight hours. The grade remained too steep for most early cars. Because reverse gear was lower than first gear, many autos were forced to back up the steeper portions of the hill. The New Mexico Highway Department frequently complained of the high cost of maintaining this two-mile stretch of road. In 1920, the grades were improved by construction of a new road bed just to the east of the old one. The new route avoided the steepest switchbacks, meeting the old grade about halfway down the hill, but plenty of hairpin turns remained. In 1932, US 85 replaced Road One, moving the main route of travel several miles to the east along the same alignment as the present I-25.

Further Reading

Atwater, Henry. "Spanish culture, religion, and trade goods flowed over the 1600-mile El Camino Real—oldest US highway." *Wild West* (February 1990).

Bourke, John G. *The Snake-Dance of the Moquis of Arizona.* 1884. Reprint. Chicago: Rio Grande Press, Inc., 1962.

Cheetham, F. T. "El Camino Militar." *New Mexico Historical Review* 15 (January 1940): 1–11.

"El Camino Real del Norte." *New Mexico Magazine* (September–October 1970): 20–23.

Moorhead, Max L. "Spanish Transportation in the Southwest, 1540–1846." *New Mexico Historical Review* 32 (April 1957): 107–22.

———. *New Mexico's Royal Road.* Norman: University of Oklahoma Press, 1958.

Chapter 13
Santa Fe Trail Ruts

■■■■■■■■■■■■■■■■■■■■■■■■■

Location: southwest of Las Vegas, New Mexico
Distance: 14 miles
Elevation: 6,400 to 6,650 feet
Elevation Change: 700 feet
Skill Level: easy
Seasons: late April to late September
Ride Surface: dirt and gravel roads
Interesting Features: Santa Fe Trail ruts
Maps: Santa Fe National Forest, USGS Ojitos Frios
     7.5-minute quadrangle

Access

● ● ● ● ● ● ● ● ● ● ● ● ● ● ● ● ●

From Santa Fe, take I-25 north toward Las Vegas. In about
fifty-five miles, exit at Romeroville, exit 339, and drive to the north
side of the interstate. Turn right, following the sign pointing toward Ojitos Frios. Parallel the interstate for a half-mile, then, as
the road turns sharply left (north) and the road surface becomes
gravel, park at the base of a ridge.

SANTA FE TRAIL RUTS

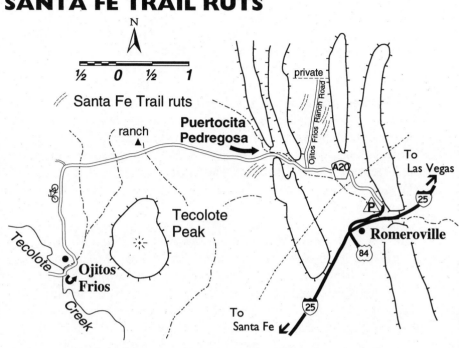

N

½ 0 ½ 1

Santa Fe Trail ruts

ranch

Puertocita
Pedregosa

Ojitos Frios Ranch Road

private

A20

To
Las Vegas

25

Tecolote
Peak

P

Romeroville

84

Tecolote Creek

Ojitos
Frios

25

To
Santa Fe

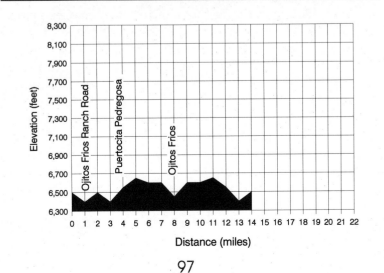

Ride Description
━ ━ ━ ━ ━ ━ ━ ━ ━ ━ ━ ━

Public access to the ruts of the Santa Fe Trail is rare. Although this ride is not much of a mountain bike route, it offers the best views of the trail in central New Mexico; this is as close as one can come to riding a section of the historic trail. Don't make the long trip to Las Vegas just to do this ride, but consider it a nice companion ride to the La Liendre tour.

Begin riding on the gravel road marked San Miguel County A20. In a quarter-mile, swing with the road as it turns left, riding between the double yellow lines of sunflowers and goldfinches. At the top of the first small hill are views of Hermit Peak to the north and Tecolote Mesa to the west. The low gap in the next ridge to the west holds the route of the Santa Fe Trail through Puertocita Pedregosa.

About one mile from the start, turn right onto Ojitos Frios Ranch Road, riding over a cattle guard and under a wooden archway. This road travels in a rural subdivision built in a long valley between two ridges, a natural route for any trail. Beyond the first few houses, ruts of the Santa Fe Trail are clearly visible on both sides of the road. Ride parallel to the Santa Fe Trail for about a half mile, then turn around at the gate marked "Road Closed."

Continue back to road A20 and turn right, following the Santa Fe Trail into a small rocky canyon, the Puertocita Pedregosa. The southern branch of the trail winds through this half-mile canyon, but the modern road has erased most of the traces of past travellers. Once through the rocky walls of the canyon, the Santa Fe Trail cuts away to the southwest. Behind a steel fence, an impressive array of deep, parallel ruts are visible climbing a low hill and disappearing over the grassy hills to the south. Continue on A20, climbing a small hill, with the ruts visible to the left as the trail heads off to the south of Tecolote Peak. In about a mile, at the top of another hill, an expansive view takes in Tecolote Peak and the grassy valley before it. In this valley, the middle branch of the Santa Fe Trail skirted the north side of the peak, and trail ruts can be seen, or at least imagined, at the base of the mesa heading toward Ojitos Frios.

At the bottom of the next hill, pass the entrance to the Tecolote Partnership Ranch. In a half-mile, the road swings left, and in another mile leads to the town of Ojitos Frios. The springs here were an important stop on the middle branch of the Santa Fe Trail. Ride slowly through the small village and admire the simple church that graces the hillside, then cross Ojitos Frios Creek and continue down a short hill to the crossing of Tecolote Creek. This crossing was probably used mostly by pack trains on the Santa Fe Trail. Stop here, enjoy the sound of the water and shade, eat a snack, then turn around and return to the car park by the same route.

Background

From 1821 until the coming of the railroad in 1879, the Santa Fe Trail was the main route into New Mexico from the "States." Trade goods and settlers traveled along the trail by mule, horseback, foot, and ox-drawn wagon. The many variations and branches of the trail coupled with a large volume of traffic left behind plentiful signs of the old road. For the modern explorer,

Ruts of the Santa Fe Trail near Fort Union, ca. 1900. (Photograph, Courtesy, Museum of New Mexico, Santa Fe, Negative No. 12845.)

ruts made by thousands of wagons as they traveled across the level plains are the most interesting remains of the old road.

Find a place along the trail where the landscape forced traffic to file through a narrow point, and ruts are sure to be found. Southwest of Las Vegas, the Santa Fe Trail turns west from its long course along the edge of the plains to cross the southern edge of the Sangre de Cristo Mountains. Only a few spots in the steep terrain offered wagons a direct route west. One such pass was Kearny Gap, a narrow slot through a ridge of tilted rock, a natural barrier to travel. The middle branch of the Santa Fe Trail passes through the gap, which is named for the American general who led his troops through the gap in 1846 during the occupation of New Mexico. After a long journey on the plains, the dramatic change in scenery near Kearny Gap always enlivened the weary travellers. Trail journals are loaded with descriptions of the crossing of the gap. Following Kearny's army through the gap, Lieutenant James Abert described the scene: "Two miles south of 'Las Vegas,' we reached a curious gate between the high escarpments of rugged granite rocks, that looked as if the surfaces had been formed by blasting with gunpowder; here, too, a little stream finds its exit from the mountains."

From Kearny Gap, the northern route was the most direct, but it led over the foothills of the Sangre de Cristos, creating difficult travel conditions for wagons or those making the journey in winter. The middle and southern branches of the main trail diverged just through Kearny Gap, each crossing the next ridge in a different place. The middle branch took a steep course over the ridge, then descended into the next valley and passed along the north flank of Tecolote Peak. The southern branch traveled up a narrow valley to cut through the ridge at a small gap, Puertocita Pedregosa. This easier route was the one used most often, as the many parallel ruts heading southwest from the gap will attest.

The narrow ridges pierced by the Santa Fe Trail are hogbacks—sharp, steeply tilting ridges of resistant rock—formed by the uplift of the Sangre de Cristo Mountains. As the mountains were pushed upward, the once-horizontal layers of sedimentary rock were broken and bent, with the layers dipping to the east, away from the uplift of the mountains. On each ridge, the tilt of the rocks creates a sharply sloping east face and forms a cliff on the west face. The streams descending from the mountains sliced through the hogbacks, creating the gaps that the Santa Fe Trail and modern roads pass through. South of Las Vegas, the rocks are from the age of dinosaurs, and although large animal fossils are rare, plant fossils, including complete tree leaves, are common.

Further Reading

Abert, James W. *New Mexico Report, 1846–1847.* 1848. Reprint. Albuquerque: Horn and Wallace, 1962.

Simmons, Mark. *Following the Santa Fe Trail.* Santa Fe: Ancient City Press, 1984.

Chapter 14
Old Bland Road
■■■■■■■■■■■■■■■■■■■■■■■■

Location: Jemez Mountains, Santa Fe National
   Forest
Distance: 18 miles
Elevation: 5,900 to 7,700 feet
Elevation Change: 2,000 feet
Skill Level: moderate
Seasons: mid-May to late October
Ride Surface: gravel roads, single track
Interesting Features: gold mining district, historic
   road, long, descending single track
Maps: Santa Fe National Forest, USGS Bland and
   Cañada 7.5-minute quadrangles

Access
● ● ● ● ● ● ● ● ● ● ● ● ● ● ● ● ●

Take I-25 to exit 264, which is about twenty miles south
of Santa Fe and thirty-five miles north of Albuquerque. Travel
west on NM 16 toward Cochiti Pueblo. In eight miles, turn right
at the T-intersection with NM 22. Follow NM 22 past the spill-
way for Cochiti Dam, but continue straight when NM 22 turns
left at the base of the dam; follow the signs to the town of Cochiti
Lake. Pass through the town and continue straight. About three
miles past Cochiti Lake, the road changes to all-weather gravel
and becomes FR 268. After one mile on the gravel road, bear right
on FR 89. Continue 1.5 miles and park under the trees along FR
89 near Dixon's Orchards.

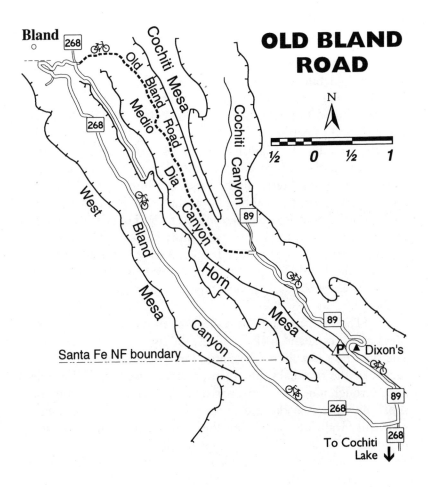

OLD BLAND
ROAD

N

½ 0 ½ 1

Bland

268

Cochiti Mesa

Old Bland Road

Medio

Dia Canyon

Cochiti Canyon

89

West

Bland

Mesa

Horn

Canyon

Mesa

89

P ▲ Dixon's

Santa Fe NF boundary

89

268

To Cochiti
Lake ↓

268

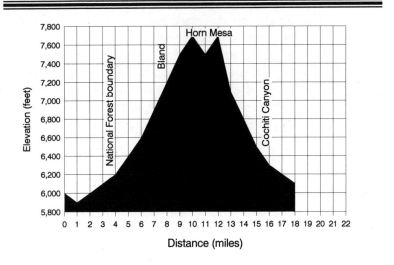

Horn Mesa

National Forest boundary

Bland

Cochiti Canyon

Elevation (feet)

Distance (miles)

Ride Description

▬ ▬ ▬ ▬ ▬ ▬ ▬ ▬ ▬ ▬ ▬ ▬

From Dixon's, backtrack up the hill on FR 89, traveling south for one mile, then turn right on FR 268. From the intersection, the tuff cliffs of Horn Mesa are seen to the right; on the very tip, six hundred feet above, sits the large ruin called Ha-Nut, the last site of the Cochiti Pueblo before it was moved to the valley after the arrival of the Spanish explorer Coronado. FR 268 climbs a low saddle, then drops into Bland Canyon. From the canyon bottom, begin the fifteen-hundred-foot climb to the top of Horn Mesa. Fortunately, the climb as far as the town of Bland is gentle and smooth. About 1.5 miles beyond the forest boundary are some small tent rocks to the right and a short narrow canyon worth exploring on foot. Eight miles from the start is the huge fence surrounding Bland. The gold mining center from the turn of the century is in remarkably good shape, but remains closed to the public.

The next half-mile is a steep climb to the top of Horn Mesa on a rutted and rocky road. At the top is a three-way fork. The right fork is a short spur onto Horn Mesa. This road is very rocky for the first half-mile, then presents a wonderful 1.5-mile glide through pine forest on a narrow ridge. Great views from the short hiking trail at the end of the road make it a perfect lunch spot. All in all, this spur from the main route is highly recommended.

From the saddle and fork atop Horn Mesa, take the fainter middle track (not the roads to Bland, Horn Mesa, or FR 268), which drops sharply past a "No Trespassing" sign. The route now follows the Old Bland Road, the first route into Bland from Albuquerque. The winding road is steep for a couple hundred yards, then becomes more gentle. At the first intersection, turn left onto the more gentle route rather than the rutted and steep straight path. Wind down the old road, through the pines, and imagine trying to get a team of horses or mules up the slope. About 1.5 miles from the top of Horn Mesa, the road reaches the bottom of Medio Dia Canyon. Follow the easy single track downstream. This is a lovely stretch of riding with water, rocks, high cliffs, and easy coasting. It is about 3.5 miles to Cochiti Canyon, with eight stream crossings on the way. At the eighth crossing (near where two streams meet), bear left a bit to pick up a gravel road.

Now in Cochiti Canyon, turn right onto FR 89 and continue coasting downhill, making a few short climbs and two more stream crossings. After a mile in Cochiti Canyon, FR 89 climbs steeply to bypass the narrowest section of the canyon bottom. Follow the shelf road for a half-mile, then descend through a series of switchbacks to the bottom of the canyon and Dixon's.

Background

Even with the modern road system, most nineteenth-century mining camps are difficult to reach. Turn time back a hundred years, and the transportation of mining equipment and supplies over narrow, twisting roads becomes a staggering feat. A bicycle ride on the winding curves of the Old Bland Road will convince anyone of the exacting skills needed to drive a wagon pulled by a team of mules from the railroad to the mountain camps.

Bland and its twin town of Albemarle got their start in the early 1880s when prospectors found promising veins of gold and silver near the head of what was then known as Pino (now Bland) Canyon. Uncertainties concerning the richness of the ores and land ownership delayed actual mining until 1889 when a tent camp was organized in the canyon. The fortunes of both towns changed in 1893 when major mines—the Ellen L., the Mammoth, and the Washington Group—were discovered in Bland Canyon, and the Albemarle group was located in Colle Canyon.

Once established, the towns boomed, drawing the title of "The New Cripple Creek" from a Denver newspaper. Although Albemarle boasted larger mines, Bland quickly became the leading community of the mining district, functioning as the supply and cultural center. The boom came so quickly that Bland was overflowing with people. The number of hotels in town was inadequate for the number of workers; tent hotels helped, but even then some miners were forced to sleep in surrounding canyons or in the town streets. It is remarkable how much town was fit into a small canyon less than one hundred feet wide. There was room only for Main Street and a single string of buildings on each side. Stores, shops, saloons, hotels, mining stamp mills and ore processing centers were all crammed onto the floor of the canyon. In some cases, the canyon walls had to be blasted away to widen the canyon and accommodate new construction.

About one million dollars worth of gold and silver was dug from the hills of the Bland district. In addition to mining, four sawmills operated in the surrounding canyons, supplying lumber not only for the towns but also for export to build a new bridge over the Rio Grande at Cochiti. By 1900, two thousand people lived in Bland, employed by mines, mills, stores, and lumber camps.

The first road into the district, the Old Bland Road, was the supply line for freight coming from the nearest railroad station at Thorton, now Domingo. The road paralleled the Rio Grande to Cochiti, then crossed the foothills of the southern Jemez Mountains to the small farming community of Cañada. The difficulty of passage increased as the road entered Cochiti Canyon and climbed a bench high above the canyon's narrowest section. Continuing upstream, and crossing the stream many times, the route turned up Medio Dia Canyon, then finished with a difficult climb over and descent from Horn Mesa. Wagons using the Old Bland Road carried lumber, mining materials, and milling equipment, and a stage line regularly bounced passengers over the canyons and mesas.

Roads into Albemarle were even more difficult. The four-mile route over the ridge between Bland and Albemarle was known as the "Teamsters' Nightmare." Built by the mining company for fifty thousand dollars, the narrow, steep, and twisting route re-

Stagecoach on Bland's Busy Main Street, ca. 1900. (Photograph by Lucien A. File, Courtesy, New Mexico State Records Center and Archives, Santa Fe, No. 12550.)

quired a round-trip climb of almost twenty-five hundred feet. Hauling heavy equipment over this road took teams of sixteen horses and considerable skill and nerve on behalf of the driver.

After almost ten years of prosperity, the end came quickly to Bland and Albemarle. In Bland, first mining faltered, then the lumber operations. As declining ore values eliminated profits, the Cochiti Mining Company shut down the mill at Albemarle in 1902, triggering a mass exodus. Two weeks after the mill closed, only about fifty people remained in the two towns.

But there is still gold in the hills. Mining continues today at the Washington Group, and Bland itself is fenced off and under guard; Albemarle remains in private hands. Riders in the Bland area should respect the rights of property owners and take care to stay off private land.

Further Reading

Jones, Fayette A. *New Mexico Mines and Minerals*. Santa Fe: New Mexico Printing Company, 1904.

Stanley, F. *The Bland, New Mexico Story*. Pep, Texas: Private printing, 1964.

PART 3

----

*Riding
the
Railroad*

Chapter 15
Chili Line I: Barranca Hill

■■■■■■■■■■■■■■■■■■

Location: west of Taos, Carson National Forest,
    Bureau of Land Management land
Distance: 25 miles
Elevation: 6,250 to 7,300 feet
Elevation Change: 1,100 feet
Skill Level: difficult
Seasons: April to May, September to November
Ride Surface: gravel roads, old railroad grade
Interesting Features: the Chili Line, scenic views
Maps: Carson National Forest, USGS Carson, Taos
    Junction, and Velarde 7.5-minute quadrangles

Access

●●●●●●●●●●●●●●●●●●

From Española, drive north on US 84/285. In five miles, turn right and follow US 285 as it splits off toward Ojo Caliente. In about one mile, turn left with US 285 at a T-intersection. Continue north through Ojo Caliente and past the junction with NM 111, which is about twenty-five miles from Española. Nine miles beyond NM 111, at Taos Junction, turn right onto NM 567, and immediately turn right again onto FR 557. Drive a short distance on this rutted dirt road and park in any of the small turnoffs. Those with a high clearance vehicle may shorten the ride by driving on FR 557 for 2.2 miles and parking at a cattle guard.

BARRANCA HILL

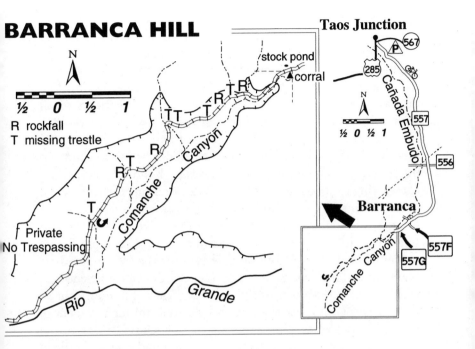

N

½ 0 ½ 1

R rockfall
T missing trestle

Private
No Trespassing

stock pond

corral

Comanche Canyon

Rio Grande

Taos Junction

285

567

P

557

556

Barranca

557F

557G

Comanche Canyon

N

½ 0 ½ 1

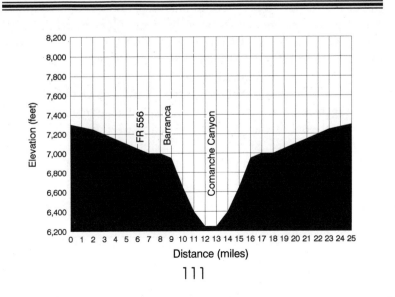

Ride Description

■■ ■■ ■■ ■■ ■■ ■■ ■■ ■■ ■■ ■■ ■■ ■■ ■

Following the abandoned Chili Line down Barranca Hill is a ride for those with a deep love of New Mexico history or those who enjoy a masochistic challenge. Fifty years have passed since the line was last used or maintained, and time has taken its toll. The grade from Taos Junction to Barranca has been converted into a forest road and is an easy haul, suitable for riders of all abilities; the route in Comanche Canyon down to near the Rio Grande is rocky and eroded, punctuated by missing trestles and huge rockfalls. Riders are forced to find a route around the missing trestles, twice carrying bikes for a hundred yards while clambering over basalt boulders. Road cuts along the route have collapsed into piles of rubble that must be crossed by pushing or carrying a bike. The easy grade of the railroad returning up Barranca Hill is misleading: the amount of time carrying a bike makes this ride a challenge suitable for only the strongest riders. Nevertheless, the vivid history and interesting engineering encountered on this ride are a powerful draw. Barranca Hill should not be missed. Those who wish to experience the route through Comanche Canyon without the difficult challenge may chose to ride to the stock pond and corral at the top of the hill and hike the railbed into the canyon.

Begin riding south on FR 557. This sandy road follows the route of the railroad as it gradually descends across flat plains of sagebrush and juniper. Look for evidence of the railroad in the form of patches of cinder showing through the sand and scattered rusted bolts and rail spikes. Few landmarks are found on this broad plain: a cattle guard just beyond mile two, and a couple of minor forest roads heading off in both directions. Just past FR 557C, look right for views of Cañada Embudo. At mile 5.5, cross a powerline and FR 556. At mile seven the road swings west to begin the drop into Cañada Embudo.

After crossing another cattle guard, the road borders a large sagebrush plain and the road surface changes to cinder. Small patches of coal at the side of the road mark the site of the rail station of Barranca. Stop for a few minutes at the intersection of FR 557F, FR 557G, and FR 557, and explore Barranca on the flat area to the north; little remains but a field of daisies, a few small foundations, and piles of rusty tin cans. A quarter-mile side trip up FR 557F leads to an expansive view of the Picuris Mountains and canyons meeting the Rio Grande Gorge below.

From Barranca, take the gravel-bedded FR 557G to the southwest. In three-quarters of a mile, the route comes to a stock pond and a corral. From this point, fences marking the border of BLM land block the route into Comanche Canyon, and the corral has obliterated the trace of the railroad. To pick up the route into the canyon, go to the far west end of the corral and climb the fence to enter a small fenced enclosure. Ride through the gap in the left (east) side of the enclosure, turn right, and parallel the fence to a lone, large juniper tree. At the juniper, turn right and pick up a cow path heading west toward a cluster of juniper trees that borders a narrow cut through the rocks about two hundred yards to the west. After about one hundred yards on the cow path, locate a raised grade bordered with rocks heading into the cut to the west. Turn left on a faint path atop the grade. Sections of this mounded route have a gravel surface, and rotted railroad ties are scattered in the sagebrush as it drops into the narrow cut blasted out of the basalt. Once in the cut, the route has an impossibly rocky bottom and seems an unlikely location for a railroad grade. Push your bike through this section and soon emerge into the very head of Comanche Canyon. Here a graded surface has obviously been built up from the canyon bottom and looks more like a railroad grade. Railroad artifacts are easily found strewn on the surface.

The route now stays in Comanche Canyon. The next obstacle, a large rockfall, is only fifty yards down canyon. Just before reaching the rocks, look on the cliff to the right for a "railroadglyph" dating from 1893. Skirt the rocks by climbing a bit to the left. Beyond the fall, the trail opens up, but riders must constantly dodge rocks, ruts, and sagebrush. Ride downhill as the grade clings to the side of the now much wider Comanche Canyon. Just before coming to a fence, look for the remains of a wooden culvert under the railbed. Continue through the gate and a roadcut to the first of the major missing trestles and the site of the 1929 derailment. Here a one-hundred-foot section of railbed is gone. Follow a hiker's trail down and to the right, carrying your bicycle over rocks for about one hundred yards. If this seems difficult, keep in mind that the route doesn't get any easier below, and consider parking here and hiking the rest of the way into the canyon.

Just down canyon is a long roadcut in which the grade is completely covered by large boulders fallen from the cliffs. This section requires another difficult *portage* of about one hundred yards. Just when it looks safe to climb on the bike again, you come to the second major missing trestle. Deeper than the first, this gap in the road requires a longer, more difficult detour to the left. Drop into the arroyo and stop at the bottom to look for huge timbers from the trestle, strewn about the rocks, and a few timbers still in place under the railroad grade. Once back on the grade, be cheered by the knowledge that the worst is over—until the return climb.

Rockfall on Barranca Hill Being Cleared by Railroad Workers and Passengers, ca. 1932. *(Photograph by George Law, Courtesy, Museum of New Mexico, Santa Fe, Negative No. 45172.)*

It is now possible to ride what will seem like long stretches of the grade. Several minor missing trestles are easily passed by walking to the right, and there are more roadcuts with small rockfalls. The route contours a side canyon, sweeping a broad turn made famous by historic photographs. This side canyon is so large that the missing trestle is easily bypassed on the hiking trail that dips into the canyon and out the other side. Pass through another large roadcut, then ride a smooth section, passing a wooden culvert with large beams still in place. Along this stretch are plenty of railroad artifacts in the form of bolts, spikes, sheet metal, wooden ties, steel plates and sections of rail. Please enjoy these relics and leave them where they are found so that the next rider may find them too.

About 3.5 miles down from the head of Comanche Canyon, a deep arroyo cuts the railroad grade. To bypass this missing trestle with a bicycle would require a supreme effort, costing energy that needs to be saved for the arduous climb back up the hill.

With private land barring the way only a half-mile farther on, this arroyo makes a logical turnaround point. Riders can explore the last half-mile by hiking around the arroyo and continuing on foot to an old fence cutting across the grade. From the fence, climb the small hill to the left to get a view of the mouth of Comanche Canyon and the Rio Grande Gorge. Do not cross the fence line onto private property as the owners do not take kindly to trespassers.

From the deep arroyo, turn around and return by the same route. On the way back, it is easy to spot the original railroad grade as it was first established in 1880. Dating from the 1920s, the newer route you have been riding on crosses small gullies atop mounds of fill; the old route contours the gullies and can be located by the small piles of rocks stacked against the hillsides. Once out of the canyon and back on the plateau, the long, gentle uphill climb back to Taos Junction is a pleasant contrast to the rock-dodging work of following the grade in Comanche Canyon.

Chapter 16
Chili Line II:
Otowi to Buckman

■■■■■■■■■■■■■■■■■■■■■■■■■■■■

Location: southwest of Santa Fe, Santa Fe National
  Forest
Distance: 8 miles
Elevation: 5,450 to 5,500 feet
Elevation Change: 100 feet
Skill Level: easy
Seasons: September to May, except after recent
  snowfalls
Ride Surface: dirt and gravel single track, sandy
  washes
Interesting Features: the Chili Line, White Rock
  Canyon, petroglyphs
Map: USGS White Rock 7.5-minute quadrangle

Access

● ● ● ● ● ● ● ● ● ● ● ● ● ● ● ● ● ●

From Santa Fe, go north on US 84/285 to Pojoaque, then
turn left on NM 502 toward Los Alamos. Continue on NM 502
about seven miles to Otowi Bridge over the Rio Grande. Cross the
bridge and park on the south side of the road near a yellow cattle
guard.

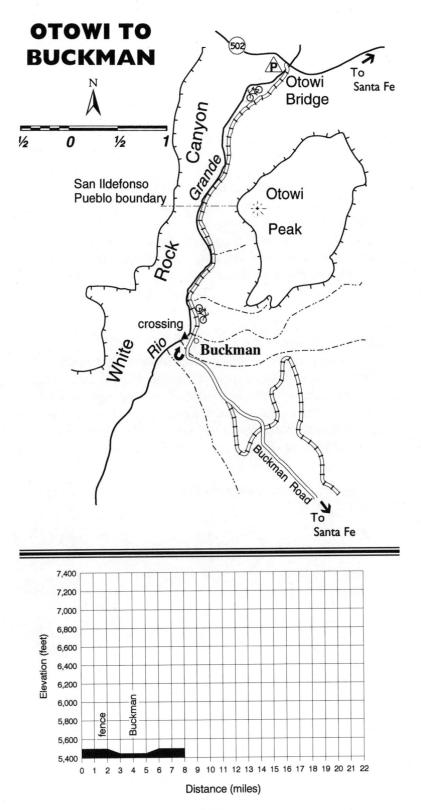

OTOWI TO BUCKMAN

N

½ 0 ½ 1

San Ildefonso
Pueblo boundary

502

P

Otowi
Bridge

To
Santa Fe

Otowi

Peak

White   Rock   Canyon

Rio   Grande

crossing

Buckman

Buckman Road

To
Santa Fe

7,400
7,200
7,000
6,800
6,600
6,400
6,200
6,000
5,800
5,600
5,400

Elevation (feet)

fence

Buckman

0 1 2 3 4 5 6 7 8 9 10 11 12 13 14 15 16 17 18 19 20 21 22

Distance (miles)

Ride Description

▬ ▬ ▬ ▬ ▬ ▬ ▬ ▬ ▬ ▬ ▬

The unusual ride to Buckman provides more of a rock-dodging obstacle course than a chance to stretch your leg muscles. The trail, which lies atop the railroad grade of the Chili Line through White Rock Canyon, is littered with basalt blocks that have fallen from the cliffs above. Twisted and brush-lined, the grade is interrupted seven times where wooden trestles once spanned small arroyos. Riders must detour into these arroyos on steep trails, and for safety it is best to walk bicycles into and out of them. Although the ride is on level ground, the many impediments and attractions lengthen the riding time for the three miles from Otowi to Buckman to about one hour.

The first mile of the ride passes through San Ildefonso Pueblo land. Hikers and bikers are permitted on Otowi Bridge and the old railroad grade, but those leaving the grade will be trespassing. To avoid problems, stay on the trail.

From the yellow cattle guard, cross the Rio Grande on the newly refurbished historic highway bridge. Pillars of the old railroad bridge can be seen just downstream. Turn right and follow the black cinder grade. In a few hundred yards, enter a willow thicket and look to the left for the footings of the water tank that once stood here. In the thicket, notice the decaying wooden cul-

The Ride Over Otowi Bridge Used To Be Much More Difficult before It Was Refurbished in 1992.

vert that protected a small trestle from water flowing down the arroyo.

Seven arroyos of various sizes must be crossed in the next half-mile. The first two arroyos are small and may be ridden across; the next four require short detours to the left. In a small road cut about a half-mile from the bridge, find small petroglyphs on the shiny basal boulders on the hill to the right. Beyond the cut, look for unusual six-sided basalt columns leaning into the hillside to the left. A small gully requiring a short *portage* marks the seventh and last missing trestle. About a hundred feet after the gully, scan the south side of the boulders above and to the left of the trail for "Kokopelli Rock," scribbled with five hump-backed flute players.

With the missing trestles behind, enjoy a long but slow run of rock dodging with the trail perched precariously above the river. About two miles from the start, cross a fence that marks the boundary of the San Ildefonso Pueblo. From here the trail is less rocky, and decaying railroad timbers can be found scattered along the trail. About a half mile after the fence, at the entrance to a grand amphitheater of volcanic cliffs, both Anasazi and historic petroglyphs are found to the left of the grade. Across a sandy arroyo, the route finally opens up and offers a short chance to stretch the legs.

Near Buckman, the railroad was forced to cross a number of deep arroyos that drain Buckman Mesa, and riding is easier off the grade. With the railroad on the right, follow a double track across a second sandy wash. In a few hundred feet there is another wash; cross the railroad and ride down this streambed toward the river. One hundred feet from the water, turn onto a narrow track to the left, riding under a tunnel of tamarisk. Cross yet another sandy arroyo, and continue to the next wash, which shares its course with a road. Turn right, riding down the road/wash to the river and Buckman's Crossing, the site of a bridge that once spanned the Rio Grande. Note that four-wheel drives have created a confusing maze of roads in this area. If you lose the route, simply continue parallel to the river until you cross the road/wash leading to the crossing. At the river, enjoy the water and soaring cliffs, and look for Buckman Road as it winds up the canyon walls across the river. Return to Otowi from Buckman by retracing the route along the railroad grade to the car park.

Background

—————————————————

Although the Atchison, Topeka and Santa Fe (AT&SF) Railroad reached New Mexico in 1877, it chose to bypass the New Mexican city in its name and brought prosperity to Albuquerque. Santa Fe was indignant to be left as just another second-class town without a railroad. However, the Denver and Rio Grande (D&RG) Railroad proposed to answer the hopes of a railroad for northern New Mexico by building a narrow gauge extension of the main D&RG line in Colorado to Santa Fe.

Construction of the Santa Fe route began at Antonito, Colorado, in 1880. The D&RG had grand visions of extending the tracks all the way to the seaport of Guaymas, Sonora, but competition with the AT&SF brought the extension to a grinding halt. Shortly after grading began, in a high-level deal with the AT&SF, the D&RG agreed not to operate more than ninety miles south of the New Mexico–Colorado border. Hence, when construction resumed, the line was forced by the agreement to end at Española, thirty miles short of Santa Fe.

Once again, Santa Fe was left without a rail connection to the rest of the nation. Seeking a local solution to the problem, a group of Santa Fe businessmen, with support from financiers in New York, incorporated the Texas, Santa Fe and Northern (TSF&N) Railway. The TSF&N sought not only to complete the thirty-mile connection to the D&RG in Española, but also to continue south, through the new gold mines at Cerrillos, to Texas. Not until 1886 did the financial situation allow the TSF&N to begin grading the line. By early 1887, TSF&N trains rumbled through White Rock Canyon, making the trip to the Española station in just over two hours.

Eventually, the D&RG's agreement with its competitors expired, allowing the D&RG to acquire control of the TSF&N. The railroad now traversed the entire Spanish-flavored backcountry along the Rio Grande, earning the track the endearing nickname "Chili Line." Steam locomotives pulled small trains of passengers and freight across northern New Mexico for sixty years. Freight consisted of lumber from the Tusas Mountains, minerals from Taos County, sheep and cattle from the ranches of the Taos Plateau, apples from the Española Valley, and, in a good year, perhaps ten carloads of piñon nuts.

On its daily passage through the lonely, open plains of the Taos Plateau and along the Rio Grande, the train was greeted as a close friend. Evidence of the casual nature of the operation is found in accounts of conductors tossing their already read morning newspaper off the train to an isolated ranch house along the line. After years of declining volumes of freight, in 1941 the line was shut down, and the tracks were torn up and sold for scrap to aid the war effort. Abandonment came a year too soon as 1942 brought the establishment of the research facility at Los Alamos and the demand for shipping large amounts of material to the remote Pajarito Plateau, practically overlooking the abandoned railroad grade.

Barranca Hill was the most famous stretch along the Chili Line. Surveyors faced the problem of finding the best route to descend twelve hundred feet from the Taos Plateau to the banks of the Rio Grande. The original planned route dropped to Pilar, providing for easy access to Taos, but cost-cutting measures forced the line to take a steeper and less expensive route down Comanche Canyon to Embudo on the river.

Barranca Hill's 4 percent grade and tight, winding turns made it the most formidable portion of the route to Santa Fe. On freight trains, ascending the hill required a double head—two engines—from Embudo to Barranca. Traveling south required a heavy reliance on the train's brakes and extreme caution on the part of the trainmen. On 17 July 1929, an engineer lost control of the downhill run on Barranca Hill. Traveling at thirty miles per hour, Engine No. 174 jumped off the trestle at mile 346, the first large span in Comanche Canyon. The engine and the first car plunged off the bridge into the arroyo below, killing the engineer and fireman, and injuring eleven others.

The D&RG built Barranca Station at the head of Comanche Canyon. In addition to a wye track for turning around helper engines after they pulled freight up the steep hill, Barranca held maintenance buildings, a coal bin, and workers' cabins. A small depot handled the few passengers and freight coming up a winding path from Glenwoody, a gold mining camp on the Rio Grande. Southbound trains stopped at Barranca to allow the brakeman to set retainers to help with slowing trains as they descended the long grade.

At the foot of Barranca Hill, Embudo Station was established as a watering stop before the long climb. Embudo also served as a passenger station, a maintenance yard for handling rail cars traveling in both directions, and a turnaround point for helper engines. Unlike other locations along the line, the station and water tank are preserved at Embudo. The buildings are not acces-

121

sible from Barranca Hill but can be visited from NM 68 in the Rio Grande Gorge.

Through upper White Rock Canyon, the Chili Line acts as the thread linking two historic sites that owed their existence to the railroad. On the north end of the canyon is Otowi, the location of a small rail station that served San Ildefonso Pueblo and the Los Alamos Ranch School, and where a frail woman from the East, Edith Warner, found a new and vibrant life in the wilds of New Mexico. At the south end of the upper canyon is the site of Buckman, a tiny town and the railhead for a lumbering operation that used the D&RG tracks to send its wood products to market.

The river crossing at Otowi is a natural route from the Sangre de Cristo Mountains to the west. The Anasazi and their Pueblo descendants used the crossing for hundreds of years before the first bridge at the site was erected by the railroad in 1887. After only two years, this first span was replaced by the iron bridge that carried the trains across the river for the next fifty-three years. The railroad recognized the importance of the Otowi crossing and permitted wagons and, later, automobiles to cross the bridge at their own risk. The railroad bridge across the Rio Grande at Otowi

The Two Bridges, Rail Station, and Edith Warner's House at Otowi, ca. 1932. (Photograph by Velma Ludlow, Courtesy, Museum of New Mexico, Santa Fe, Negative No. 21180.)

is now gone, sold in 1942 for scrap metal to assist in the war effort.

As automobile and freight traffic increased, the New Mexico State Highway Department saw the need to construct a vehicle bridge across the Rio Grande at Otowi. In 1924, the original Otowi Bridge, a suspension span ten feet wide and 175 feet long, was opened for public use. The bridge carried cars heading for the pueblo ruins and guest lodge in Frijoles Canyon, and to the newly opened Los Alamos Ranch School at the top of the hill. This bridge still spans the Rio Grande downstream from the modern four-lane bridge. The old bridge was refurbished by the New Mexico Highway Department in 1992.

In 1942, the Los Alamos Ranch School was transformed into a secret town for developing the world's first nuclear weapons. Suddenly, the vehicle bridge at Otowi was too small to handle the hundreds of truckloads of freight headed up the hill. Heavy trucks coming from the railhead at Lamy, south of Santa Fe, had to detour to Española to cross the river. When the war was over and Los Alamos became a permanent research facility, a new bridge was built at Otowi to accommodate the heavier traffic. The second bridge was in use until 1988 when it was dismantled after the current four-lane bridge was erected.

Otowi's lasting fame can be attributed to Edith Warner who lived at the crossing from 1931 until her death in 1952. Searching for a way to earn a meager living that would allow her to stay in New Mexico, Warner accepted a position as freight handler for the Los Alamos Ranch School. She supplemented this income with a gas pump and a small tea room that served tourists visiting the plateau. Her gentle nature and quiet friendliness won her the confidence of railroad men, visitors, many of the people of San Ildefonso Pueblo, and later, scientists working on the Hill. For the physicists racing to beat Germany to the secrets of the atomic bomb, Edith Warner's tea room became a tiny haven where they could escape from the pressures of their work.

Another outsider, Henry Buckman, arrived in New Mexico from Oregon in 1898. In contrast to Warner, who drew spiritual strength from the river and the landscape, Buckman sought to exploit the easy access to the ponderosa pine forests of the Pajarito Plateau brought by the Chili Line. He quickly acquired the timber rights from the owners of the Jose Ramon Vigil Grant and started to build a lumber empire. The center of operations, the town of Buckman, was located where the Chili Line left White Rock Canyon and began the long uphill haul to Santa Fe. On the edge of

Pajarito Canyon, just northwest of the present town of Los Alamos, he constructed a sawmill. Buckman bridged the Rio Grande and built a steep, winding road up the plateau to connect the mill and the town. Armed with contracts from markets in Denver, Buckman worked the forests, shipping his entire output of lumber up the D&RG to Colorado. By 1903, Buckman had some serious trouble with his creditors, hastily sold his operations in New Mexico, and fled to California with the profits.

Further Reading

Chappell, Gordon. *To Santa Fe by Narrow Gauge: The D&RG's "Chili Line."* 1969. Reprinted from *Colorado Rail Annual.* No. 7. Golden, Colorado: Colorado Railroad Museum, 1988.

Church, Peggy Pond. *The House at Otowi Bridge.* Albuquerque: University of New Mexico Press, 1960.

Gjevre, John A. *Chili Line: The Narrow Rail Trail to Santa Fe.* Española: Rio Grande Sun Press, 1971.

Rothman, Hal. *On Rims and Ridges: The Los Alamos Area Since 1880.* Lincoln: University of Nebraska Press, 1992.

Chapter 17
Santa Fe Northwestern Railway

■■■■■■■■■■■■■■■■■■■■■■■■■■■■■■■

Location: Jemez Mountains, Santa Fe National
Forest
Distance: 10 miles
Elevation: 7,200 to 7,600 feet
Elevation Change: 400 feet
Skill Level: easy
Seasons: mid-May to late October
Ride Surface: dirt and gravel roads
Interesting Features: old railroad grade, fossils
Maps: Santa Fe National Forest, USGS San Miguel
Mountain 7.5-minute quadrangle

Access

From San Ysidro, travel NM 4 eight miles north to the junction with FR 376 at Cañones. Turn left onto FR 376 and follow the road past Cañones and Gilman about five miles to the Guadalupe Tunnels. Stop and explore the tunnels, then continue on FR 376 as the pavement ends and the surface becomes all-weather gravel. Continue seven miles to the junction with FR 539 at Porter. Do not cross the bridge over the Rio Guadalupe; park at the junction on the left side of FR 539. Riders who wish to extend this ride can begin riding at the tunnels to increase the route to twenty-four miles.

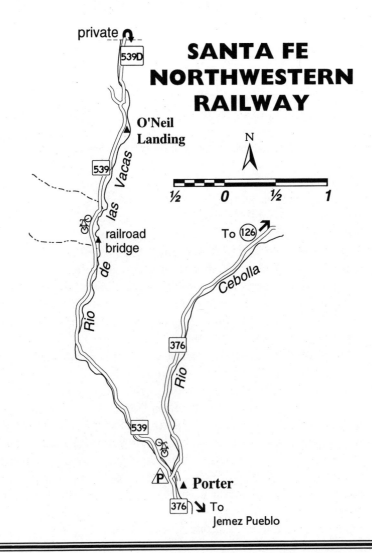

SANTA FE
NORTHWESTERN
RAILWAY

private

539D

O'Neil
Landing

539

Rio de las Vacas

railroad
bridge

N

½   0   ½   1

To 126

Cebolla

376

Rio

539

P ▲ Porter

376 ↘ To
Jemez Pueblo

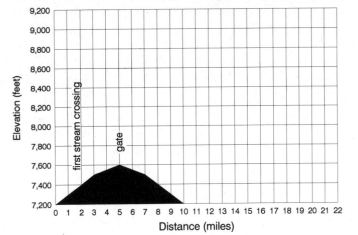

Chapter 17

Ride Description

━━━━━━━━━━━━━

FR 539 parallels the Rio de las Vacas and roughly follows the grade of the Santa Fe Northwestern Railway (SFNW). Although the road is bumpy, the gentle slope and short distance, coupled with abundant railroad artifacts, make this ride suitable for families. Plan on making a day of it: stop at the Guadalupe Tunnels, explore the railroad grade by bicycle, and try your skill at landing a few trout from either the Rio de las Vacas or the Rio Guadalupe. Along the bike route are plenty of places at streamside that make ideal rest or lunch spots.

The junction of FR 376 and FR 539 lies at the railroad town of Porter. Before or after the ride, spend a few minutes exploring the flats on the other side of the Rio Guadalupe. Few signs remain of the large railroad operation that once stood there: outlines of foundations, twisted chunks of rusted steel, and a single stone chimney from an old cabin.

Riding the SFNW is a game of careful observation. In the narrowest sections of the canyon the road lies directly on top of the old railroad grade; but for most of the way, the grade follows a slightly different course than the road. After the first crossing of the Rio de las Vacas, it is possible to follow visually almost the entire railroad as it crosses and recrosses both the road and the Las Vacas. To know exactly where the grade lies will challenge your powers of observation and attention to detail. The grade is easiest to locate in any of the numerous meadows along the stream. Look for the railroad as it cuts through small hills and the modern road climbs around them. Long, linear raised mounds are another sign of the grade. Here is a further hint: if not beneath the modern road, the railroad is usually between the road and the stream.

To play the game, simply follow FR 539, the left fork of the intersection, west from Porter. The road is often highly rutted but is easy riding; three wet crossings of the Rio de las Vacas add to the fun. About 3.5 miles from Porter, take the right fork, FR 539D, and continue another half-mile to a gate at the boundary of private land. Turn around at the gate and return by the same route.

A few features should not be missed. The small limestone cliffs along the road hold abundant fossils of sea life. At many places along the grade, railroad ties can be found in place—even on the forest road. There are several opportunities for leaving the forest road and riding the actual railbed. About one mile up from the second crossing of the Rio de las Vacas, be sure to take a short spur road leading down to a meadow along the stream. In this meadow are an intact section of a bridge across the Las Vacas, and, downstream one hundred yards from the bridge, a dugout section of railbed with at least a dozen ties still in place. About three miles up from Porter is a broad meadow on both sides of the Las Vacas, the site of the logging and railroad camp of O'Neil Landing.

Background

The Santa Fe Northwestern (SFNW) Railway was incorporated in 1920 to make use of 425 million board feet of ponderosa pine lying on the Cañon San Diego Grant in the western Jemez Mountains. Timber rights for the grant were held by Guy Porter. In 1922, Porter formed the White Pine Lumber Company and built a sawmill at Bernalillo. In November of that year, railroad construction began.

Grading the SFNW was an easy task from the mill at Bernalillo up the Jemez River Valley and the Rio Guadalupe to the Guadalupe Box. At the box, the railroad was forced to find a route through a huge block of hard granite. The canyon carved by the river was too narrow to follow, so the engineers decided to blast two tunnels through the granite high above the level of the river. Although less than a half-mile long, grading the stretch of the SFNW through the Guadalupe Box cost one-half million dollars, half the cost of the entire railroad.

The first shipments of logs to the mill were delivered in September 1924. Most of the logging was done in side canyons above the box, and logs were skidded by horses to flat areas along the stream to load onto the railroad cars. Loaded trains made the easy, downhill trip from Deer Creek to Bernalillo in about three hours. Hauling empty trains back up through the box required "doubling the hill," making two half-size trips from below the box to Deer Creek.

By 1925, the timber in the Deer Creek drainage had been exhausted, and the SFNW expanded up the Guadalupe to its head at the junction of the Rio Cebolla and the Rio de las Vacas. A flat area at the new railhead was large enough for a logging and railroad camp. The company built warehouses, a small railyard, wye tracks, sidings, and a store, and gave the new camp the name of Porter. Within a year, three hundred people lived at the camp, mostly in cabins in the surrounding forest. The railroad continued its smooth operations. The forty-mile run from Bernalillo to the box took about three-and-a-half hours; the seven miles from the box to Porter took almost an hour-and-a-half.

As timber vanished from the Cañon San Diego Grant, the White Pine Lumber Company looked to the surrounding Santa Fe National Forest. In 1930, the company secured timber rights for the Cebolla and Las Vacas watersheds. From Porter, the company pushed railroad and lumber operations up the Rio Cebolla as far as Fenton Lake. By 1933, when this timber was also gone, it was necessary to tear up the track up the Cebolla and lay it along the Rio de las Vacas. The SFNW expanded about six miles up the Las Vacas to Ojitos Camp. Along the new line, the company had access to a huge tract of timber in the National Forest. In 1937, Porter was abandoned and operations were moved up the Las Vacas to O'Neil Landing.

A high volume of timber was shipped by rail out of the mountains from O'Neil Landing through 1941. In May of that year, heavy rains washed away three miles of track between the Guadalupe Box and O'Neil Landing. With damage estimates exceeding one hundred thousand dollars, the company decided to abandon the railroad and convert its hauling operations to trucks. Over the next several years, the rails were torn up, the railroad grade was converted to a truck road, and the tunnels were enlarged to accommodate logging trucks. A new sawmill was constructed on the flats near Gilman, just below the Guadalupe Box. Logging by road continued in the Guadalupe watershed until 1973.

Railroad and Lumbering Facilities at Porter, New Mexico, September 3, 1930. (Photograph by J. D. Jones, United States Department of Agriculture, Forest Service, Photograph No. 249031.)

Further Reading

Glover, Vernon. *Jemez Mountain Railroads, Santa Fe National Forest, New Mexico*. Santa Fe: Historical Society of New Mexico, 1990.

PART 4

■■■■■■■■■■■■

Volcanoes, Mines, Rocks, and Minerals

Chapter 18
Cerros del Rio I: Chino Mesa

■■■■■■■■■■■■■■■■■■■■■■■■

Location: west of Santa Fe, Santa Fe National Forest
Distance: 23 miles
Elevation: 6,300 to 6,750 feet
Elevation Change: 1,200 feet
Skill Level: moderate
Seasons: in light snow years, all winter, March to
      June, September to December
Ride Surface: dirt roads, rutted double track
Interesting Features: volcanoes, Montoso maar,
      scenic views
Maps: USGS Montoso Peak and White Rock 7.5-
      minute quadrangles

Access

● ● ● ● ● ● ● ● ● ● ● ● ● ● ● ● ● ●

From the intersection of Cerrillos Road and Saint Francis Drive in Santa Fe, take Saint Francis (US 84/285) north for one mile to West Alameda. Turn left on Alameda, which becomes Santa Fe County Route 70. In four miles, the pavement ends, and the surface becomes all-weather gravel. Wind past homes and many side roads, always staying on County Road 70. One-and-a-half miles past the end of the pavement, bear left (still on CR 70); 2.5 miles past the end of the pavement, bear right under a powerline onto FR 24. Pass under another powerline and over a cattle guard at five miles from the pavement. The fence here marks the boundary of the Santa Fe National Forest, and the road becomes rutted dirt, passable with caution in any vehicle. Cross two more cattle guards, the third 1.6 miles from the forest boundary. Four-tenths of a mile past the third cattle guard, park to the left where a faint road and fence go west up a hillside.

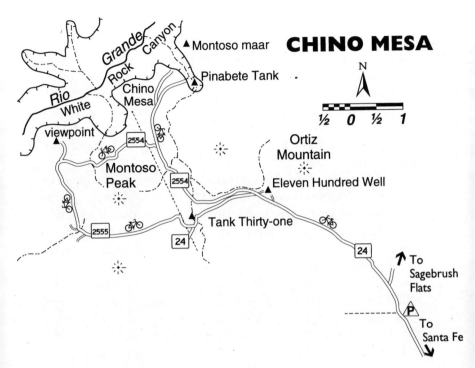

CHINO MESA

N

½ 0 ½ 1

Montoso maar
Pinabete Tank
Rio Grande
Rock Canyon
White
Chino Mesa
viewpoint
2554
Montoso Peak
2554
Ortiz Mountain
Eleven Hundred Well
2555
Tank Thirty-one
24
24
To Sagebrush Flats
P
To Santa Fe

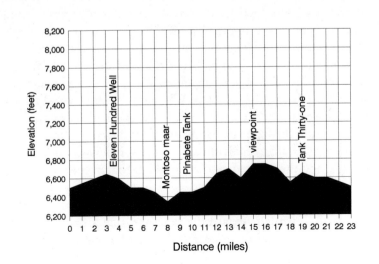

Elevation (feet)

8,200
8,000
7,800
7,600
7,400
7,200
7,000
6,800
6,600
6,400
6,200

Eleven Hundred Well
Montoso maar
Pinabete Tank
viewpoint
Tank Thirty-one

0 1 2 3 4 5 6 7 8 9 10 11 12 13 14 15 16 17 18 19 20 21 22 23

Distance (miles)

Ride Description

▬ ▬ ▬ ▬ ▬ ▬ ▬ ▬ ▬ ▬ ▬

For mountain bike riders, the Cerros del Rio area is an undiscovered paradise. Semi-wild, laced with seldom-used jeep trails winding between eroded volcanoes, the Cerros area offers many days of exploring potential. Within the field, every hill is an old volcano, the long ridges are the edges of lava flows, and the ground is covered with volcanic cinders and bombs. The hard lavas cap the rims of White Rock Canyon, and views from the canyon edge are spectacular.

The Cerros del Rio volcanic field is crossed by a maze of both well-maintained and fading roads. Even with sketch maps and a detailed written route description, it is impossible to anticipate all the wrong turns riders may make in this area. It is imperative that riders in the Cerros del Rio area carry topographic maps to help them navigate.

From the car park, continue in the same direction (north) on FR 24. In one mile, pass the intersection with the road to Sagebrush Flats, continuing straight ahead. FR 24 gradually swings to the west, skirting the southern flanks of Ortiz Mountain. Four miles from the start, pass a short spur road right, leading to a corral and Eleven Hundred Well. Near the corral, the mesa on the right is composed of lava from the Ortiz volcano, and each hill in sight is a lobe of a lava flow. Less than a half-mile past the corral, bear right onto FR 2554. Descend gradually toward a powerline and small arroyo at the foot of Montoso Peak, ignoring the many side roads.

Ride two miles on FR 2554. Shortly after crossing a second rocky arroyo, FR 2554 bears left. For now, just note this intersection: the route returns to FR 2554 after a spur to Chino Mesa. Continue straight, gently descending for about a mile, and past the sign and road for Pinabete Tank. In another half-mile, the road fades near the edge of a canyon. Park here and walk to the rim where a magnificent view of White Rock Canyon and the Rio Grande awaits. The viewpoint is perched on the rim of a side canyon that cuts through the Montoso maar. From above, the buff water deposits, many individual lava flows, reddish soils baked by hot lava, and the congealed basalt of the throat of the maar can be seen.

From the viewpoint, backtrack a half-mile to the Pinabete Tank road. Turn left toward the tank and ride a half-mile, stopping where the road fades near the head of a narrow canyon. A faint stock trail leads down into the canyon, which is best explored on foot. Visible from the trail is the algae-colored Pinabete Tank, a series of small tinajas scoured out of the basalt floor of the canyon. Search the cool canyon for the fir trees for which the tank was named. Exploring a short distance downstream is worth the effort.

Return to the main Chino Mesa road and retrace the route south for a half-mile until reaching the intersection with FR 2554 passed earlier. Turn right (west), ride under and then parallel to the powerline for a short distance, then turn left on a rutted double track heading west. This rocky jeep road skirts the base of Montoso Peak, the high volcano to the south. Follow this road about three miles as it rounds Montoso Peak and approaches the edge of White Rock Canyon. Turn right at a prominent T-intersection and ride this short spur about a half-mile to the end. A walk of one hundred yards west from the end of the road leads to another viewpoint of White Rock Canyon. While walking, search the red cinders covering the ground for small volcanic bombs thrown from Montoso Peak during its last eruptions.

From the viewpoint, backtrack past the road around the base of Montoso Peak and continue south on a very rutted road. In 1.5 miles, pass a side road from the right, then go through a gate to a Y-intersection. Turn left onto FR 2555, climbing a low saddle at the base of Montoso Peak. From the saddle, ride downhill to a powerline, turn right to parallel the powerline for a short distance, then follow the road as it turns left away from the powerline. In a hundred yards, turn left at the intersection with FR 24. In a mile, pass where this route turned onto FR 2554, and continue to backtrack four miles to the car park.

Chapter 19
Cerros del Rio II: Twenty-nine Volcano Loop

∎∎∎∎∎∎∎∎∎∎∎∎∎∎∎∎∎∎∎∎∎∎∎∎∎∎∎∎∎∎

Location: west of Santa Fe, Santa Fe National Forest
Distance: 27 miles
Elevation: 6,400 to 7,200 feet
Elevation Change: 1,800 feet
Skill Level: difficult
Seasons: in light snow years, all winter, March to May, September to December
Ride Surface: dirt roads and rutted double tracks
Interesting Features: volcanoes, scenic views
Maps: USGS Agua Fria and Montoso Peak 7.5-minute quadrangles

Access
● ● ● ● ● ● ● ● ● ● ● ● ● ● ● ● ● ●

From the intersection of Cerrillos Road and Saint Francis Drive in Santa Fe, take Saint Francis (US 84/285) north for one mile to West Alameda. Turn left on Alameda, which becomes Santa Fe County Route 70. In four miles the pavement ends and the surface becomes all-weather gravel. Wind past homes and many side roads, always staying on County Road 70. One-and-a-half miles past the end of the pavement, bear left (still on CR 70); 2.5 miles past the end of the pavement, bear right under a powerline onto FR 24. Pass under another powerline and over a cattle guard at five miles from the pavement. The fence here marks the boundary of the Santa Fe National Forest, and the road becomes rutted dirt, passable with caution in any vehicle. Cross two more cattle guards, the third 1.6 miles from the forest boundary. Four-tenths of a mile past the third cattle guard, park to the left where a faint road and fence go west up a hillside.

138

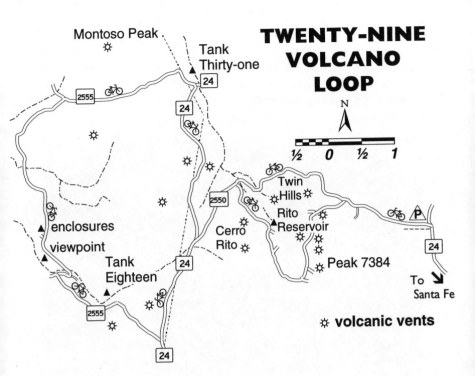

TWENTY-NINE VOLCANO LOOP

Montoso Peak

Tank Thirty-one

N

½ 0 ½ 1

Twin Hills

Rito Reservoir

enclosures

viewpoint

Cerro Rito

Tank Eighteen

Peak 7384

To Santa Fe

☼ volcanic vents

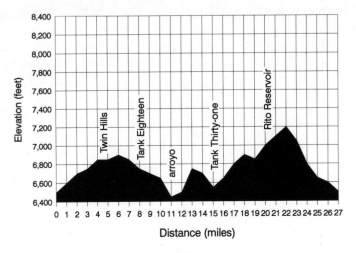

Ride Description

▬ ▬ ▬ ▬ ▬ ▬ ▬ ▬ ▬ ▬

This sprawling figure-eight loop will take you through the heart of the Cerros del Rio volcanic field. Start counting volcanoes at the beginning of the ride: the loop passes within sight of twenty-nine of them. Because of the confusing maze of roads found here, be certain to carry the topographic maps of the area.

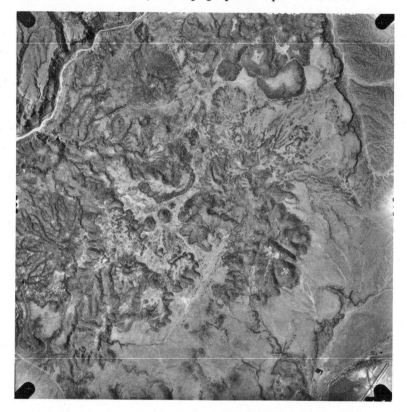

High-altitude Aerial Photograph of the Cerros del Rio Volcanic Field. *(EROS Photograph, Courtesy, United States Geological Survey.)*

Begin riding on any of the several tracks heading west parallel to the fence on the left (west) side of FR 24. Climb gradually on any of the rutted dirt roads, which gradually merge into one. Ride toward the Twin Hills, passing a number of side roads in both directions. In about two miles, the return route of this loop comes in from the left; continue straight on the less-used road that climbs uphill. As you approach the Twin Hills, look left to find a line of rock domes composed of basalt. Each dome is the site of a volcanic vent with hardened lava congealed in its throat.

The road climbs a small divide and skirts the north flank of the Twin Hills, where the road surface is covered with red cinders and fist-sized blocks of scoria. The road turns rocky and drops across two small arroyos. Immediately after crossing the second arroyo, continue straight, but note this intersection: the loop returns to this point later in the ride.

Continue on this road, now identified as FR 2550, for one mile to the intersection with FR 24, which is about six miles from the start. Turn left on FR 24, and soon cross under a powerline. Continue downhill toward Colorado Peak to the south. After 1.5 miles on FR 24, turn right onto FR 2555 as FR 24 goes left under the powerline. In a few hundred yards, take the right fork, descending between two small volcanoes and passing Tank Eighteen. Next comes a mile of bumpy downhill. One-and-a-half miles below Tank Eighteen the route enters an open area where a small arroyo comes in from the right. At a group of some small slump pits along the arroyo, look for a faint road to the right. (If the road you are on becomes a cow path heading into a narrowing canyon, backtrack a hundred yards and search for the pits and the faint road.) Turn northeast across the open area and ride about three hundred yards to an alternate route from Tank Eighteen. Turn left. In a half-mile the road reaches the top of a rise with a magnificent view of the San Miguel Mountains and Capulin and Alamo canyons across the Rio Grande.

Shortly after the viewpoint is an obscure intersection near a cluster of small wire enclosures. Bear right on a faint trail to the north. The route soon becomes more distinct as it begins a sometimes rocky drop into a small canyon. About 1.5 miles from the enclosures, cross an arroyo and climb 1.5 miles to a road coming in from the left at the base of Montoso Peak. At this intersection, continue straight, climbing a low saddle, then dropping to a powerline and FR 24.

Turn right onto FR 24, gradually climbing to a saddle between two small volcanic cones. During the climb the route is literally surrounded by volcanic vents: every hill and mound in the 360-degree view is an extinct volcano. After 2.5 miles on FR 24, turn sharply left onto FR 2550, which was traveled earlier in the opposite direction. In a mile, at the arroyo at the foot of the Twin Hills noted before, bear right and climb a moderate hill on the road now cut through eroded basalt flows. After the route levels, watch for a deeply cut canyon on the left. A short walk to the canyon edge will reveal the inner structure of a lava flow from the Twin Hills, exposed as the stream carved the small canyon. Notice how the lava on top of the flow differs from that near the bottom. Volcanic bombs litter the surface here, and from this vantage point one can make out the outline of the crater on top of the nearest of the Twin Hills.

Continue up a small valley, passing Rito Reservoir on the left, and Cerro Rito on the right. The route climbs out of the valley and winds its way to a broad ridgetop. Just over a mile from Rito Reservoir is a prominent intersection. Bear left, riding a quarter-mile to the base of the highest basalt knob in the area, peak 7384 on the Montoso Peak quadrangle. It is worth the effort to climb the knob and enjoy the 360-degree view. (Be on the watch for rattlesnakes in warm weather.)

Continue past Peak 7384, winding between the basalt remains of more volcanic vents. Drop down a very steep, gravelly hill: don't hesitate to walk this one. At the base of the hill, pass a faint road to the left and continue straight. A half-mile from the base of the hill, turn right onto the road on which the ride began. Descend about two miles to the car park.

Background

—————————————

From the remote edge of Chino Mesa, the serene hills and smooth-flowing Rio Grande deep within White Rock Canyon create a tranquil scene. The view belies the location of the Cerros del Rio volcanic field in the middle of one of the great splits in the earth's crust; the landscape spreading in all directions was born of the most powerful forces on the planet.

Although the outside of the earth seems like a solid shell, the crust is actually broken into about two dozen massive pieces called plates. Sliding around on plastic rocks about forty miles below the surface, the plates are driven by currents within the earth. On the continents, we rarely notice any of this slow-motion change unless we are near the edge of a plate where two bump and grind, or slide over or under one another. Most geological excitement—earthquakes and volcanic eruptions—occurs along plate boundaries.

For the past forty or fifty million years, the western United States has been at the leading edge of the North American plate as its westward motion forces the Pacific plate to slide under the continent. As can easily be imagined, the consequences of such massive earth-play can be far reaching. The lifting of the Rocky Mountains, the cracking and rising of the island mountain ranges from Albuquerque to Reno, Nevada, California's well-documented San Andreas Fault, and unnumbered thousands of volcanic vents are all a direct result of plate crunching.

Earth-shattering events are hard to envision from the placid rim of an isolated canyon in northern New Mexico. However, stretching from north to south, even farther than the view from Chino Mesa, the sliding of plates has activated an ancient crack in the continent of North America. As magma, the molten rock found in the upper layers of the inner earth, rises toward the surface of New Mexico, the heat stretches the surface, pulling it apart. The stretching has created huge cracks—faults—and between the faults the surface has dropped as much as twenty-six thousand feet!

The Rio Grande rift extends from Poncha Pass in Colorado south to El Paso, splitting New Mexico in half. Without sand, gravels, and rocks washing in from the Sangre de Cristo and other mountain ranges bordering the rift, and a number of extensive piles of lava filling up the rift zone, central New Mexico would be a deep, steep-walled valley such as the similarly formed East Africa rift.

Fifteen million years ago, the area of White Rock Canyon looked much like the broad plains surrounding Albuquerque, with no gorge, no plateaus above the river, and even no Jemez Mountains. As volcanic activity began, the ancestral Jemez Mountains rose to the west. About two-and-a-half million years ago, the faults close to the Rio Grande tapped a source of magma, and the first of the Cerros del Rio volcanoes was born. Early eruptions in the field produced small cinder cones—piles of small bits of lava shot out of a volcanic vent. As the composition of the hot rock coming up from the inner earth changed, the eruptions turned quiet, oozing fluid lava in great quantities, piling flow after flow into thick sheets. This lava cooled to form basalt—a dark, dense rock speckled with tiny holes left behind by escaping gases. Later eruptions from the same vents again formed cinder cones; these are the hills of the Cerros today. The cones, such as the Twin Hills, are in excellent condition after two million years of erosion, probably because they were long protected by thick blankets of pumice and ash from the largest Jemez Volcano across the river. This huge mountain, whose activity began about the time the Cerros field ended its eruptive phase, blew apart about one million years ago, forming the Valle Grande caldera and spewing out massive amounts of volcanic ash.

After a million years of volcanic activity, the once broad valley of the Rio Grande was filled with a huge pile of volcanic rock. Numerous times, the river was dammed by lava flows, creating great lakes in the valley. Each time, the river sliced a path through the lava dam and continued cutting the canyon. Today, the Rio Grande Gorge cuts through one thousand feet of rock.

Scoria and Two Volcanic Bomb Fragments with Breadcrust Appearance.

What comes out of a volcanic vent—the opening from which volcanic materials emerge—can take a variety of forms, dependent on the gas content of the magma and the size of the particles. The smallest bits of lava, shattered into dust-sized bits by violent, gassy eruptions, are called volcanic ash. Larger pieces, from sand to pebble size, are known as cinders. Scoria is any cinder covered and filled with thousands of gas holes. The largest chunks of lava thrown from a vent are volcanic bombs. Fist- to boulder-sized, bombs are shot high enough to cool partially on the way down, forming a distinctly streaked "breadcrust" shell that makes them easy to pick out in a field of volcanic rock.

One unusual feature of the Cerros del Rio field is the concentration of volcanic maars, explosive craters formed when hot magma meets cold groundwater. Because many of the vents of the Cerros field are located near the Rio Grande, the chances of water and magma meeting were great. As hot rock rising in a vent came into contact with water, the instant conversion of the water into steam created small but violent explosions. The view from the rim of Chino Mesa includes a cross section of the Montoso maar across a small side canyon.

Further Reading

Aubele, Jayne. "The Cerros del Rio Volcanic Field." In *New Mexico Geological Society Guidebook, 30th Field Conference, Santa Fe County.* Socorro: New Mexico Geological Society, 1979.

Chapter 20
El Malpais and the Big Tubes
■■■■■■■■■■■■■■■■■■■■■■

Location: south of Grants, El Malpais National
   Monument
Distance: 17 miles
Elevation: 7,600 to 7,900 feet
Elevation Change: 400 feet
Skill Level: easy
Seasons: dry spells from mid-April to June,
   September to November
Ride Surface: gravel and dirt roads
Interesting Features: cinder cones, lava tubes,
   "fresh" lava flows
Maps: USGS Cerro Hueco and Ice Caves 7.5-
   minute quadrangles

Access
● ● ● ● ● ● ● ● ● ● ● ● ● ● ● ● ● ●

   From the west side of Grants, take exit 89 of I-40, NM
53. Go south twenty-six miles to about one mile past the entrance
to Bandera Crater and Ice Caves. Turn left on County Road 42.
Drive about one-quarter mile and park in a wide turnout on the
left side of the road.

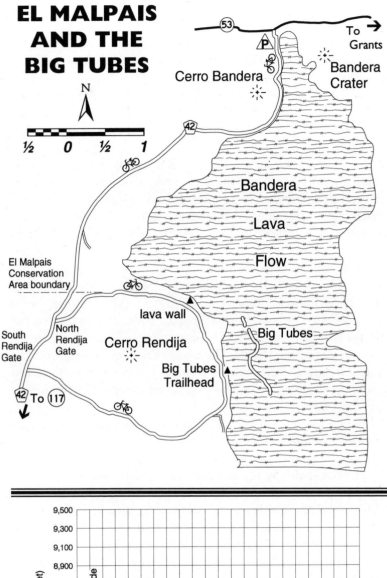

EL MALPAIS AND THE BIG TUBES

N

½ 0 ½ 1

To Grants

53

Cerro Bandera

Bandera Crater

42

Bandera

Lava

Flow

El Malpais
Conservation
Area boundary

lava wall

Cerro Rendija

Big Tubes

South
Rendija
Gate

North
Rendija
Gate

Big Tubes
Trailhead

42 To 117

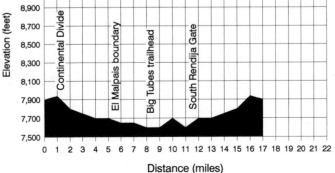

Elevation (feet)

9,500
9,300
9,100
8,900
8,700
8,500
8,300
8,100
7,900
7,700
7,500

Continental Divide

El Malpais boundary

Big Tubes trailhead

South Rendija Gate

0 1 2 3 4 5 6 7 8 9 10 11 12 13 14 15 16 17 18 19 20 21 22

Distance (miles)

Ride Description

■■■■■■■■■■■■■

CR 42 is notorious for being impassable when wet. After rains, the surface is sticky and difficult to travel; huge puddles, including one known locally as "The Monster," linger for weeks in low areas. Before starting out on this ride, make certain the surface is dry. Check at the El Malpais Information Center in Grants (620 East Santa Fe Avenue, (505) 285 5406) for the latest information.

Visitors should not visit the Big Tubes area without venturing into at least one of the lava tubes. To enjoy the Big Tubes area fully, be prepared to go underground. Mountain bike riders need to carry some unusual equipment: sturdy hiking boots, heavy work gloves, and three sources of light—perhaps a lantern, flashlight, and a candle with some matches. A bike helmet easily doubles for head protection inside a lava tube.

The ride to the Big Tubes area begins heading south on CR 42. As the road threads a narrow passage between Cerro Bandera on the right and the edge of the Bandera lava flow on the left, the crest of the first small hill is more significant than it seems: it is the Continental Divide. The Bandera flow originated from the base of Bandera Crater, which is visible just beyond the flow. Excellent opportunities to explore a fresh lava field are found for the next 1.5 miles.

CR 42 is an easy ride until the road turns away from Bandera flow and heads out over older lavas. For weeks after heavy rains, the next three miles form a string of puddles. Biking around the puddles is sloppy but presents no problem, and the mud certainly helps keep down the number of vehicles using the road. Observe the "Private Property" signs along this section.

Riding south, the Chain of Craters extends on the right from the low mounds just west of the road to the dominating cone, Cerro Americano, ahead. On the left is Cerro Rendija; the Big Tubes area is on the back side of this massive cone. About five miles into the ride, cross a cattle guard at the El Malpais boundary. A half-mile beyond the boundary, turn left at the North Rendija Gate onto a double track marked as recommended for four-wheel drive. Follow the four-wheel drive road around the north side of Cerro Rendija. After a mile, the Bandera flow again comes into view. Two miles from the north gate, the edge of the flow is over fifty feet high and is worth exploring. On the surface of this flow, all the features of unweathered lava flows—aa, pahoehoe, squeeze-ups, and sinkholes—can be found.

Continue circling Cerro Rendija for almost another mile to a short spur that is marked for the Big Tubes area. Park and lock bicycles here, and explore on foot. The trail to the lava tubes is marked with large cairns. Begin at the signpost and locate the first cairn to the east. Walk to the cairn, then sight the next one before moving on. Continue in this manner to the lava tubes. Be prepared to spend at least an hour exploring the tubes and the lava flow, then return to your bicycle by the same route.

Continue riding around the back side of Cerro Rendija, ignoring several side roads to the left. Pass the skeleton of a 1950s vintage car, and ride over a collapsed lava tube located about one mile from the Big Tube area. About four miles from the Big Tubes, rejoin CR 42 at the South Rendija Gate. Turn right, passing the north gate in a half-mile, and continue back to the car park on CR 42.

Background

Children are easily captivated by two aspects of geology: dinosaurs and volcanoes. Many of us subconsciously carry these first loves into adulthood. For the volcano-loving child in all of us, there is El Malpais National Monument and Conservation Area.

El Malpais is the scene of New Mexico's most recent volcanic activity. The many cinder cones and lava flows of the area are geologically young, all under one million years old, and the McCarty's flow, which can be seen along the interstate just east of Grants, is certainly less than one thousand and perhaps as young as four hundred years old. With hundreds of square miles of volcanic landscape, the plains south and east of the Zuñi Mountains are without a doubt the best place in the state to enjoy the features of basalt flows.

Important to understanding volcanoes is the fact that they exhibit two basic types of eruptive activity. Volcanoes with silica-rich, sticky, gas-trapping lava tend to have explosive eruptions: Mt. St. Helens in Washington is a recent example. Volcanoes of Hawaii are the best example of the other, quiet type of eruption: glowing red streams of fluid rock cascading along and covering everything in their path. The rock formed when the latter type of lava cools is usually black basalt. El Malpais lavas are almost exclusively basalt, an indication of quiet eruptions from the dozens of volcanic vents on the field.

Cinder cones are small piles of pebble-sized bits of lava spit out during the early history of a volcanic vent. Large amounts of pressurized gases are mixed in with the magma, causing it to be fractured and thrown into the air. The cone is formed as the bits pile up around the source. Most of the round hills in El Malpais are cinder cones: Bandera Crater, Cerro Bandera, El Calderon, and the Chain of Craters are some prominent examples.

As the gas content of the lava drops, cinder production falls and the now-fluid lava simply oozes from the vent either to pool in the crater of the cinder cone or spread out over the surrounding terrain. The lavas of El Malpais were extremely fluid, some flowing over twenty miles from their source.

Older lavas close to a million years in age underlie the soils of the western part of this ride. The Bandera flow is much younger—certainly under ten thousand years—and exhibits all of the features of fresh basalt flows. A walk over the surface of the flow will reveal different textures of the rock. Rough, jagged lava is given the Hawaiian word *aa*. Smooth, ropy lava with graceful curved lines is termed pahoehoe. Squeeze-ups are split mounds of lava formed when an obstruction stops the forward motion of the flow and the continued pressure of the lava forces the flow into a low mound.

The most fascinating features of the El Malpais lava flows are lava tubes, long tunnels worming under the surface. As lava flows away from its source, the surface in contact with the much colder air cools and thickens faster than the lava below. A crust may form on top of the flow, while the lava below remains fluid. If

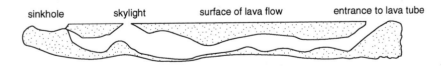

sinkhole   skylight   surface of lava flow   entrance to lava tube

Cross Section of a Lava Tube

the supply of lava is shut off at the source, the last of the flow may drain from beneath the crust, leaving behind a subsurface passage. When a section of the roof falls into the tube, an entry into the tunnel is created. Later, the entire tube will collapse, forming a chain of sinkholes.

The Big Tubes caves are part of a lava tube system in the Bandera flow. The flow, which emanated from a breach in the south wall of Bandera Crater, extends twenty-five miles, all the way to Grants. The lava tube system begins just outside the south wall of the crater and can be traced over twelve miles through the flow. Much of the tube has collapsed to form sinkholes, examples of which can be seen in the Big Tubes area. Dozens of small, disconnected tubes remain intact, offering riders willing to get off their bikes a full day of exploration. At the Information Center, be sure to pick up the National Park Service brochure on the Big Tubes area, which includes a detailed map of the interior of the largest caves.

Further Reading

Maxwell, Charles. *Geologic Map of El Malpais Lava Field and Surrounding Areas, Cibola County, New Mexico.* United States Geological Survey Miscellaneous Investigations Series. Washington, D.C.: Government Printing Office, 1986.

Jarita Mesa Mines
■■■■■■■■■■■■■■■■■■■■■■■■■ .

Location: northwest of Española, Carson National
   Forest
Distance: 15 miles
Elevation: 8,000 to 8,800 feet
Elevation Change: 1,100 feet
Skill Level: moderate
Seasons: May through October
Ride Surface: gravel and dirt roads
Interesting Features: minerals, mines, scenic views
Maps: Carson National Forest, USGS Las Tables 7.5-
   minute quadrangle

Access
● ● ● ● ● ● ● ● ● ● ● ● ● ● ● ● ●

From Española, travel five miles north on US 84/285. Turn
right onto US 285, heading toward Ojo Caliente. In one mile, the
road turns left and continues around the foot of Black Mesa. About
twenty-five miles north of Española, pass through the town of
Ojo Caliente. One-and-a-half miles north of Ojo Caliente, turn
left on NM 111 toward La Madera and Vallecitos. In five miles,
pass through La Madera, continuing on NM 111; after fifteen
miles, pass Vallecitos. Three miles beyond Vallecitos, turn right
onto the graded gravel FR 45. In dry weather, this road is passable
with any vehicle. Climb 3.5 miles to the top of Jarita Mesa, and
park at the junction with FR 110 near a sign marked for US Highway 64.

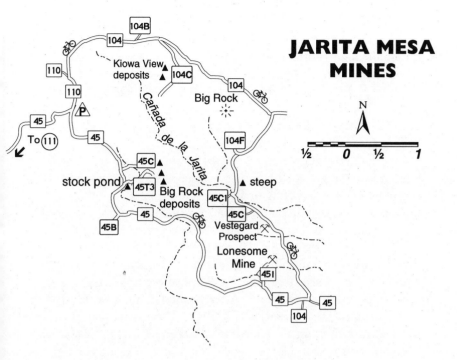

JARITA MESA MINES

104B
104
Kiowa View deposits ▲
▲ 104C
104
Big Rock
110
110
P
45
To (111)
45
104F
Cañada de la Jarita
45C ▲
▲
stock pond ▲ 45T3
Big Rock deposits
▲ steep
45C1
45C
Vestegard Prospect
45B
45
Lonesome Mine
45I
45
45
104

N

½ 0 ½ 1

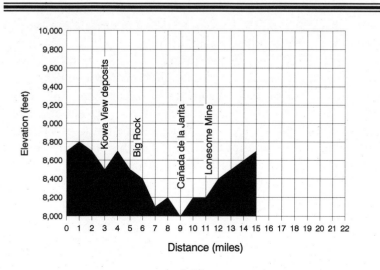

Ride Description

▬ ▬ ▬ ▬ ▬ ▬ ▬ ▬ ▬ ▬

The ride on Jarita Mesa is a mineral collecting trip by mountain bike. With several stops to locate mines and mineral specimens, riders should allow four to six hours for the fifteen-mile loop. Exploring Jarita Mesa makes an excellent family outing. The ride is short and has plenty of pretty rocks to look at along the way. Except for the steep descent into Cañada de la Jarita, the route is an easy one.

Collecting a specimen or two of kyanite can be challenging, and carrying a rock hammer will help. Anyone interested in sampling mica, microcline or kyanite should be aware that scattered prospects remain on the mesa, and riders should keep out of any posted, active claims.

Begin riding on FR 110, the left fork of the intersection at the car park. In a half-mile, turn right at the junction with FR 104, and soon pass a sign marked "Big Rock, three miles, Dead End, four miles." (Ignore the sign.) After about 1.5 miles on FR 104, pass a road to the left marked FR 104B. About one-quarter mile beyond, turn right on a double track marked FR 104C. Gradually descend, looking for a large, jagged outcrop of rock on the right. In about a half-mile, park near the fork in the road where two knobs of rock are visible to the right. The knobs are the Kiowa View kyanite deposits.

Explore this area on foot, circling and climbing the knobs for 360-degree views. The rocks themselves hold thin metamorphic bands, veins of quartz, and shiny mica flecks; also look for orange, purple, pink and aqua schists. Evidence of a kyanite mining operation is found at the base of the northern knob.

Backtrack on FR 104C to FR 104 and turn right, continuing on the road as it skirts around the base of Big Rock. About 1.5 miles from FR 104C, come to a junction marked Dead End. Turn right on the road heading south. In a half-mile, where the southeast extension of Big Rock looms to the right of the road, watch for pink-veined quartz on the road, and a small vein of almost pure quartz about fifty feet to the left of the road. As the road drops a bit, come to a Y-intersection. The right fork is marked FR 104F; take the unmarked left fork and begin to drop into the Cañada de la Jarita. The descent is gentle at first, then, just past a fence line, it gets very steep. Use caution on this rutted and rocky stretch of the route. Before coming to the canyon bottom, pass a huge, swirling outcrop of metamorphic gneiss on the left.

At the bottom of the hill cross a small grassy meadow and the Cañada de la Jarita. On the south bank, pick up the road as it angles to the right. In a hundred yards, come to an intersection. To the right is marked FR 45C1; turn left and start climbing out of the canyon. At the top of the first hill, pass FR 45C on the right. About a quarter-mile from FR 45C, near a spur road to the right that has been blocked off with a dirt berm, look carefully to the right for a short boundary post standing in a pile of rocks. Walk to the post and explore the pegmatite at the Vestegard Prospect, where the ground is covered with beautiful specimens of mica, quartz, feldspar, and microcline.

Continue on the road, soon passing FR 1040 to the left, and then crossing two small drainages. In another mile, a small prospect sits on the roadside. In a quarter-mile, come to the junction with FR 45 and turn right. Continue straight on FR 45 as FR 104 turns off to the left, and begin a slow climb. In a half-mile, look for a double track angling off to the right. Turn on this road, FR 45I, and ride a half-mile to the Lonesome Mine, located on the right. USE CAUTION exploring this area: there are three open mine shafts at the site, each partially filled or blocked off with pine logs, and the sides of the shafts are unstable. The Lonesome Mine is located in pegmatite, and large chunks of quartz and feldspar, as well as palm-sized sheets of mica, are found throughout the area.

Return to FR 45, continuing west and climbing gradually. About three miles past the Lonesome Mine, pass FR 45B on the left. In another mile, just past a cattle guard and a stock pond on the right, turn right onto a double track, marked FR 45T3, leading out to a meadow. Take the track on the right side of the meadow, and head toward the prominent rock knobs ahead. Follow the track around to the base of the largest rock and explore the Big Rock kyanite deposit. Again, use caution as there are mine shafts in the area. At the northern end of the deposit are huge deposits of quartz and easily recognizable veins of blue kyanite crystals. Kyanite crystals can be found on the ground, in the cliff face, and as a blue tint in masses of schist.

Return to FR 45, and continue, passing FR 45C on the right. Reach the car park about 1.5 miles past the Big Rock deposits.

Background

Early in our academic careers we learn about three basic types of rocks: igneous, sedimentary, and metamorphic. By the time we reach seventh grade and the fourth hearing of the types-of-rocks lecture, we have some understanding of how rocks can be formed by cooling lava or by deposition by water. The mysterious process of metamorphism, occurring deep within the earth, out of sight, with unimaginable heat and pressure, is a more difficult concept to grasp.

Take a huge chunk of the earth's surface and bury it a mile or two under accumulating sediments, then perhaps grind a couple continents together nearby. Given such circumstances, it is not difficult to visualize the tremendous forces acting on rock deep within the earth's crust. The sheer weight of overlying sediments squeezes the buried rock, creating conditions of extreme heat and pressure that may partially melt the rock. Under intense pressure, strange things that even geologists only partially understand can happen. Atoms from the old rocks are mobilized, aligning themselves along pressure lines, or recombining into new minerals. Rocks are transformed into new types, such as schist—a mica-rich rock composed of thin, wavy, parallel mineral layers.

Some minerals require extreme heat and pressure to form and so are found only in metamorphic rocks. One such mineral, kyanite, is found in clusters of radiating, bladed crystals. Long crystals are valued by mineral collectors for their exquisite shades of blue. In the past, kyanite was mined for grinding into mullite, a component of ceramics and spark plugs.

Jarita Mesa is part of the Tusas Mountains, a huge mound of metamorphic rocks in north-central New Mexico. Originally, the rocks on the mesa were sedimentary rocks, changed by heat and pressure into quartzite and schist. Six large kyanite deposits are found within the schist on the mesa. The deposits are thick, blocky masses that typically jut up as knobs or ridges as much as 115 feet high. Easily recognized examples include the Kiowa View and Big Rock deposits. In the 1920s, kyanite was mined at the north end of the Big Rock deposit and operator Philip Hoyt shipped fifteen hundred tons of ore to St. Louis.

The Tusas Mountains are the site of another type of mining. The rocks of Jarita Mesa date from the Precambrian era. Metamorphic rocks of this age are often associated with an unusual type of granite called pegmatite. Under intense heat and pressure, minerals can slowly concentrate in favorable locations, allowing crystals to grow to enormous size. Huge blocks of quartz, feldspar, and mica—the minerals from which granite is made—are formed. If present, the slow cooling also permits more rare minerals to form large crystals. Pegmatites can be mined for mica, feldspar, and rarer minerals. Thick books of mica—a group of minerals with crystals easily separated into thin, transparent sheets—are not unusual in such rocks. Feldspar, usually of the va-

Quartz, Microcline, and Mica Specimens from the Vestegard Prospect on Jarita Mesa.

riety orthoclase, is a very common rock-forming mineral used in making enamel, porcelain, and glass. A typical rare mineral found in pegmatite is beryl, a blue to green silicate sometimes occurring in gem quality when it goes by the name of emerald—but this variety is not found in the Tusas Mountains.

Mica mining has a long history in the Tusas Mountains, dating from the 1700s, when clear sheets of the mineral were quarried and shipped to Santa Fe and other Spanish villages for use as window panes. In 1870, large-scale commercial mining of mica began near Cribbenville, a small settlement southeast of Jarita Mesa. Mica from at least a dozen mines was shipped by wagon to Pueblo, Colorado, where it was used to make windows for wood-burning stoves. The development of electricity and the demand for mica as an insulator in light bulbs and radio tubes brought a new wave of mining beginning in 1912. Many of the mines were reworked during the Second World War when mica was in high demand by the Army for use in communications and aircraft spark plugs.

Looking to sell mica to the military, A. B. Vestegard opened a small mine on Jarita Mesa in 1942, digging a trench twenty-five feet long, ten feet wide, and eight feet deep. Vestegard successfully extracted not only mica, but also beryl and feldspar. However, the deposit was small and profits were limited. Later, the prospect was unsuccessfully worked for beryllium, a component of beryl and a metal used in making alloys. Today, the Vestegard Prospect is known for its beautiful, pale blue-green microcline, a variety of feldspar. Fine mineral specimens of microcline, quartz and mica are easily found on the ground surrounding the prospect.

The Lonesome Mine was opened in 1932. During the war-time mica boom, the Lonesome was bought by Charles Besre who developed the extensive works found at the site today. Besre sank a deep mine shaft and two inclines, producing 130 pounds of sheet mica and 30 tons of scrap mica. Some of the sheet mica was found in books over twenty inches in diameter. Six-inch specimens of mica can still be found on the surface surrounding the shafts.

Further Reading

Corey, Allen Frank. *Kyanite Deposits in the Petaca District, Rio Arriba County, New Mexico.* Socorro: New Mexico Bureau of Mines and Mineral Resources, 1960.

Jahns, Richard H. *Mica Deposits of the Petaca District, Rio Arriba County, New Mexico.* Socorro: New Mexico Bureau of Mines and Mineral Resources, 1946.

Rim Vista

■ ■ ■ ■ ■ ■ ■ ■ ■ ■ ■ ■ ■ ■ ■ ■ ■

Location: northwest of Española, Carson National
Forest
Distance: 31 miles
Elevation: 7,600 to 8,050 feet
Elevation Change: 1,000 feet
Skill Level: difficult
Seasons: dry spells from mid-April to November, hot
in summer, best in spring and fall
Ride Surface: dirt roads
Interesting Features: scenic views, solitude
Maps: Carson National Forest, USGS Alire, Echo
Amphitheater, and Navajo Peak 7.5-minute
quadrangles

Access

● ● ● ● ● ● ● ● ● ● ● ● ● ● ● ● ● ●

From Española, take US 84/285 north. Continue straight
on US 84 when US 285 splits off to the north, passing Abiquiu, the
Ghost Ranch Visitor Center and Echo Amphitheater. Seven miles
past Echo Amphitheater, about forty miles from Española, turn
left onto FR 145, immediately passing a ranch gate. (FR 145 can
be very slick in wet weather; travel only when dry, and use caution.) Stay on the road, traveling 2.3 miles across private land to
the Berryman Ranch. Drive by the ranch house and continue
straight through a gate in the ranch yard. Immediately turn left
and continue on FR 145. Pass another ranch house on the right,
then bear right with the road. The Carson National Forest boundary is five miles from the highway; at six miles the road bears left.
Park at the intersection of FR 131 and FR 145, 6.7 miles from the
highway.

RIM VISTA

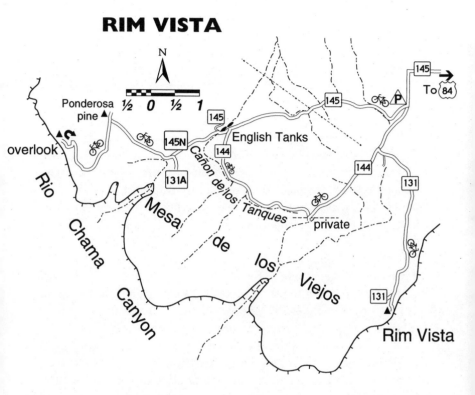

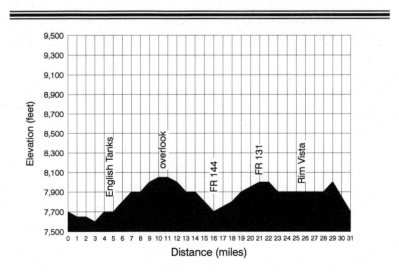

Ride Description

▬ ▬ ▬ ▬ ▬ ▬ ▬ ▬ ▬ ▬ ▬

The remote wilds of the Mesa de los Viejos offer mountain bike riders solitude like few other places in New Mexico. The highlights of this rambling route are two overlooks of the Rio Chama Canyon. The wild nature of this tour dictates all riders carry the topographic maps for the area.

Begin riding on FR 145, heading toward English Tanks. The route travels through open ponderosa pine forest on a small ridge that seems to be the top of the world. Continue downhill, ignoring the many roads that lead off in both directions. Cross under a powerline, then ride across a broad sagebrush plain offering views of mesas and the San Juan Mountains to the north. Four miles from the start, drop down to the English Tanks. Pass FR 144 on the left, and skirt around the second tank. After a 180-degree turn, bear left onto a primitive road, FR 145N. Climb the rutted dirt road for over a mile to the top of the hill where FR 131A goes off to the left; continue straight on FR 145N. Climb another small hill into open ponderosa pine woods, then descend, alternately riding through sagebrush and open woodland.

Seven-and-a-half miles from the start, where a large ponderosa pine stands at the edge of a sagebrush plain, FR 145N bears right, but take the unmarked double track that heads to the left. Climb slowly, swinging west and then following the twists and turns of the road. Three miles from the turnoff at the large pine, the road descends to the rim of Chama Canyon. Ride to the end of the road and enjoy the view.

From the vista, backtrack three miles to the large ponderosa pine, then turn right to retrace the route on FR 145N. Continue back past FR 131A, past the first English Tank to FR 144. Turn right, climbing slowly into Cañon de los Tanques. One mile past the tanks, pass a corral on the right; after two more miles of climbing, pass another ranch gate and follow as the road bears left. Soon after a short, moderate climb, turn right toward Rim Vista on FR 131. The four miles to the rim are rolling sagebrush hills. As the rim comes in sight, turn left on the marked FR 131A and ride a hundred yards to the edge of the world.

After enjoying the view, retrace the route back to the intersection of FR 131 and FR 144. Continue straight on FR 131 toward US 84, descending quickly the last 1.5 miles to the car park.

Background

Sedimentary rocks are the product of the earth recycling materials on a grand scale. Most are made from broken bits of other rocks—sand grains, clay particles, pebbles—that have been carried by wind or water and dropped in a new location. As more and more material accumulates, forming layer on top of layer, the materials are compressed and cemented, gradually producing new rock.

The Colorado Plateau is an immense block of sedimentary rock extending from Utah to New Mexico. During the last forty million years, the plateau has been uplifted over two miles. Modern streams have deeply carved their way into the rocks of the plateau, exposing thick layers of sedimentary rocks deposited by rivers, oceans, and winds throughout the age of the dinosaurs, 225 to 66 million years ago. Characterized by colorful horizontal layers, the Colorado Plateau is home of the desert West's grandest scenery.

The northwest corner of New Mexico is part of the southernmost extension of the Colorado Plateau. A few miles north of Abiquiu on US 84, the red rocks of the plateau literally jump up from beneath the surface along a great fault, a crack in the earth's surface where movement of rocks can occur. Beyond the fault and extending to the state line, bands of rock dominate the scenery. From either of the vistas atop the Mesa de los Viejos, the view encompasses over 150 million years of earth history.

While traveling through time may not be possible, rocks allow us to peek at conditions found in the past. From bottom to top, from oldest to youngest, the sedimentary rocks of New Mexico's Colorado Plateau tell a tale of rivers, deserts, lakes, and shallow oceans.

The story begins at the level of the Rio Chama and Abiquiu Lake in a broad valley cut into easily eroded red mudstones of the Chinle Formation. Clues found here—fossil trees, dinosaur bones, red clay—tell of a huge floodplain extending from central Arizona to west Texas. The red muds, composed of iron-stained clay particles, were carried by slow-moving rivers and left on broad mudflats, much like conditions on the vast floodplain of the Yangtze River today. Over time, forces from deep within the earth raised the level of the land, modified the climate, and completely changed this corner of the world. Mudflats were replaced by an extensive sand dune desert rivaling the modern Sahara. Windblown sands piled as deep as five hundred feet from New Mexico into Utah. Sweeping lines within yellowish Entrada sandstone reflect the accumulation of layer after layer of quartz grains over millions of years.

Next, a shallow, salty lake covered northwestern New Mexico, then evaporated away, leaving behind the gray gypsum of the Todilto Formation. In a somewhat wetter climate, more stream-born muds were deposited on another floodplain, creating the purple-gray slopes of the Morrison Formation. We have no record of the next forty million years, indicating either that no new rocks were formed, or that those that were formed were quickly eroded away. After this unconformity—a break in the rock sequence—a shallow sea encroached from the southeast. The sands of the shoreline left behind the sandstones of the Dakota Formation. The top layer of rocks, Mancos shale, is mud from the bottom of the sea. Today, the soft shale is easily broken down to form open plains covered with sagebrush, and yields a sticky, gloppy mud that makes travel on the roads of the Mesa de los Viejos hazardous when wet.

From the rims above the Chama Canyon, this pageant of rocks creates glorious scenery. The remote first vista along this ride offers a unique view of the canyon. Below the overlook, the Rio Chama, the force that cut through and exposed the colorful rocks, is audible as it flows out of a narrow stretch and crosses cultivated flats. At the mid-section of the opposite wall of the canyon, the yellow Entrada sandstone, capped by the gray Todilto, forms a prominent cliff that can be traced throughout the main and side canyons like a snaking bathtub ring. Above the Entrada cliff are softly forested slopes on Morrison muds. A prow of cliff-forming Dakota sandstone is directly across the canyon, and the distant skyline is composed of still younger rocks of the Mesa Verde Formation, formed by the river deltas and swampy jungles to the west of the Mancos sea shoreline.

Rim Vista

Canyon of the Rio Chama with the Entrada Sandstone Cliff at
Mid-section.

Further Reading

Muehlberger, William R., and Sally Muehlberger. *Española—Chama—
Taos: A Climb Through Time*. Socorro: New Mexico Bureau of Mines and
Mineral Resources, 1982.

Chapter 23
Fairy Crosses in Arroyo Hondo

■■■■■■■■■■■■■■■■■■■■■■■■■■■■■■■

Location: south of Taos, Carson National Forest
Distance: 10 miles
Elevation: 6,900 to 8,400 feet
Elevation Change: 1,500 feet
Skill Level: moderate
Seasons: mid-May through October
Ride Surface: gravel and dirt roads
Interesting Features: minerals, rocks, quiet canyon
    scenery
Maps: Carson National Forest, USGS Taos SW 7.5-
    minute quadrangle

Access

● ● ● ● ● ● ● ● ● ● ● ● ● ● ● ● ● ●

    From Santa Fe, take US 84/285 north to Española. At the intersection with NM 68, bear right onto NM 68 north. Continue through Velarde, past Embudo and Pilar, which is twenty-eight miles from Española. About 4.5 miles from Pilar, at the bottom of a long hill descending to Arroyo Hondo, turn right onto FR 606. Park off the road near the highway. Coming from the north, FR 606 is about ten miles south of Ranchos de Taos on NM 68.

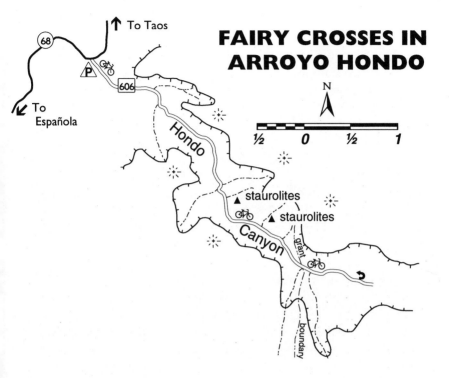

FAIRY CROSSES IN ARROYO HONDO

To Taos

68

To Española

P

606

Hondo

N

½   0   ½   1

▲ staurolites

▲ staurolites

Canyon

grant

boundary

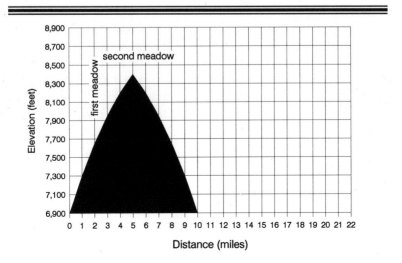

8,900
8,700
8,500
8,300
8,100
7,900
7,700
7,500
7,300
7,100
6,900

Elevation (feet)

first meadow

second meadow

0 1 2 3 4 5 6 7 8 9 10 11 12 13 14 15 16 17 18 19 20 21 22

Distance (miles)

Ride Description

The old road up Arroyo Hondo is a gentle but steady climb through a narrow canyon sliced out of the metamorphic rocks of the Picuris Mountains. The first mile is rocky and may be difficult for beginning riders, but beyond the ride is easy and pleasant. The route also offers plenty of wet stream crossings to splash through. As the canyon can get hot in summer, riders will want to start early in the day.

Begin riding on FR 606, which is identified as such only on the Carson National Forest map and never by a sign. The road quickly drops to and crosses the arroyo bottom, then begins the long but gradual climb. By the half-mile point, the canyon has narrowed, with high cliffs of quartzite and schist on both sides of the road. Above a small intake for a pipe that carries water over a nearby divide, a small stream parallels the road.

Continue the rocky climb, making many shallow stream crossings. At about 1.5 miles, ride through a large gate. As the road passes through patches of fir forest and clusters of wildflowers, the surface becomes smoother. About 2.5 miles from the start, the canyon opens up as side valleys enter from both the north and south. About halfway through this large meadow, park and explore the shallow wash entering from the left. The sandy bottom is filled with speckled rocks holding large metamorphic minerals.

Up the canyon from the meadow, staurolite crystals are common. Continue climbing, and stop and explore any of the numerous roads and side drainages that head off from the canyon bottom and lead to signs of staurolite diggings. Look for crystals in gravel beds and in outcrops of shiny mica schists. As an added attraction, red garnets dot the surface of many rocks.

Just under four miles from the start, the road crosses a fence line onto private property. In 1992, the road was not posted, but note that the landowner may restrict access at any time. If the road is open, continue another mile into a large meadow, which makes an excellent lunch stop and turnaround point. Return to the car park by the same route.

Background

To the nongeologist, the distinction between rocks and minerals may seem fuzzy. Like adobe bricks to a wall, minerals are the building blocks of rocks, the raw materials that, when mixed in different combinations, make up the hundreds of different rock types found in the earth's crust.

Because of their beauty, minerals are considered the earth's treasures. The attraction of most mineral species stems from their brilliant luster or exquisite color; but some mineral types are equally beautiful solely on the basis of shape. Staurolite is one such mineral. The crystals of this species are dull, mottled tan and brown, and yet they are prized by collectors. The secret is that staurolite is often found in symmetrical twin crystals, piercing each other in the center, forming tiny rock crosses.

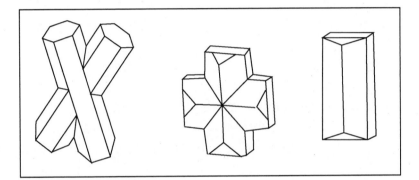

Typical Staurolite Crystals from Arroyo Hondo

Staurolite is found only in aluminum-rich metamorphic rocks. Its occurrence in large twinned crystals is limited to a few locations in North America and Europe, and specimens from the Pilar area are found in museum collections throughout the world. Large twinned staurolite crystals have long been collected and sold by dealers and curio shops as "Fairy Crosses." The Penitente Brotherhood held the mineral in special reverence, each wearing the cross as an amulet and to demonstrate his faith. Local legend adds to the lore of the staurolite: when the fairies heard of the crucifixion of Christ, they cried in anguish. Their falling tears were transformed into the crystals shaped like crosses as they struck the ground.

Further Reading

Northrup, Stuart. *Minerals of New Mexico.* 2d ed. Albuquerque: University of New Mexico Press, 1959.

Window Rock

■■■■■■■■■■■■■■■■■■■

Location: north of Española, Santa Fe National
  Forest
Distance: 11 miles
Elevation: 5,800 to 6,300 feet
Elevation Change: 500 feet
Skill Level: moderate
Seasons: dry spells in winter, March to mid-May,
  mid-September to November
Ride Surface: sandy arroyo bottom, cattle trails,
  double track, dirt road
Interesting Features: natural arch, scenic views
Maps: USGS Chili and Mendenales 7.5-minute
  quadrangles

Access

● ● ● ● ● ● ● ● ● ● ● ● ● ● ● ● ●

From Española, take US 84/285 north. In five miles, pass the intersection with US 285 north and continue straight on US 84 toward Abiquiu. Five miles past the intersection with US 285, or one-half mile past milepost 200, look for a small gate on the left (south) side of the highway. The gate is marked with a small U.S. Forest Service sign. Pass through the gate and park about one-hundred yards farther, at the intersection with the first dirt road to the left, which is directly under a powerline.

WINDOW ROCK

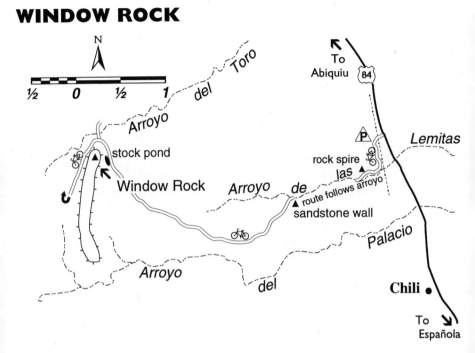

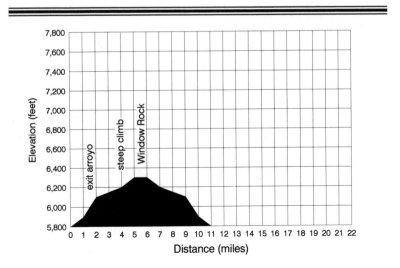

Ride Description

■ ■ ■ ■ ■ ■ ■ ■ ■ ■ ■ ■

Begin riding east along the road under the powerline. In just under a half-mile, the road enters a broad arroyo and turns right along the wash bottom. Ride the sandy track up the Arroyo de las Lemitas, heading toward a lone sandstone spire. The road ends near the spire at a green water tank. For the next mile, the route continues up the sandy arroyo bottom and riding is difficult—sometimes impossible. Riding the edges of the arroyo or on the many cow paths can make traveling easier; when all else fails, push your bike. The walls of the Arroyo de las Lemitas are composed of loosely cemented sandstone—the source of the deep sand in the arroyo bottom. Look for sculptured patterns in the rock, as well as numerous odd-shaped globs of cemented sand.

After a mile in the arroyo bottom (it only seems much longer), just past some modern "petroglyphs" carved into a sandstone wall, the canyon narrows and abruptly turns right. Exit the arroyo on an obvious road climbing steeply to the left. After the road climbs out of the arroyo, riding becomes easier, although in places it is steep and rocky.

For the next mile, the road continues a moderate climb before leveling out on a broad ridge. Follow the road as it skirts to the left of the head of the Arroyo de las Lemitas. Next comes a murderous short climb up a rocky slope. From the top of this ridge, drop gently into a broad valley. As the road crosses the valley, look for Window Rock high on the ridge to the south.

For a closer look at the arch, follow the road across the meadow past a stock pond, and cross the shoulder of the ridge holding Window Rock. Immediately turn left and ride the road on the backside of the ridge for a half-mile. The arch is not visible from the road, but can be reached by climbing the slope and searching the ridge line. After finding Window Rock, return to the car park by the same route.

Background

— — — — — — — — — —

Who can explain the fascination people have for holes in rocks? Discover an outcrop of sandstone or lava with a hole through it, and instantly hundreds of seekers will make a pilgrimage to the spot. Is it the symbolism of seeing heavenly light passing through solid rock that draws us to arches? Or are we simply attracted by the unusual, seeking the novel in the natural world? Whatever the reason, natural arches make wonderful destinations on a mountain bike.

The delicate balance of forces necessary to create natural arches makes them rare, but in the American Southwest, the abundance of naked and cracked sandstone produces a concentration of arches unlike any other region on earth. New Mexico's largest arch is Coyote Arch on the Navajo Reservation; the best known arch in the state is La Ventana south of Grants. Hidden away in quiet corners of New Mexico are dozens of lesser-known holes in the rocks.

In spite of their magical aura, arches and windows have the most common of origins. A zone of weakness in the rock—along fractures or at the boundary between two rock layers—is enlarged by weathering, the process of rotting or breaking down of rock by mechanical means. Breakdown can occur when a tree root wedges into a crack in a rock, during a freeze-thaw cycle, or by chemical solution when rocks are partially dissolved by water. As weathering weakens a rock, gravity can pull large chunks to the ground, enlarging a simple crack into a hole. If the opening forms in a thin wall of rock, an arch is born.

Window Rock

Rock openings go by the names of *arch, window,* or *natural bridge.* In the strictest sense, natural bridges are spans of rock formed by water cutting beneath them, but arch and window are used interchangeably. Probably half of the arches in New Mexico go by the generic name of Window Rock. The Window Rock in the northern Jemez Mountains is an unusual arch found not in sandstone, but in volcanic rock. The hole pierces a ridge formed when subsurface lava was squeezed into a crack in the existing rock. The cooled lava is much harder than the surrounding sandstone. As erosion washed away the overlying layers, the sandstone was carried away, leaving behind a narrow ridge of resistant lava. Many years after the ridge was exposed, the arch formed and was enlarged. The fifteen-foot opening through the ridge is high on the skyline and is visible from miles away. Window Rock is best appreciated by taking the short but steep climb to the arch from the north side of the ridge.

Further Reading

Barnes, Fran. *Arches and Bridges*. Moab, Utah: Canyon Country Publications, 1987.

Chapter 25
Teakettle Rock
■■■■■■■■■■■■■■■■■■■■■

Location: west of Los Alamos, Santa Fe National
 Forest
Distance: 30 miles
Elevation: 8,100 to 9,100 feet
Elevation Change: 3000 feet
Skill Level: difficult
Seasons: dry spells May through October
Ride Surface: gravel and dirt roads
Interesting Features: natural arch, ruins, wild mesa
 and canyon scenery
Maps: Santa Fe National Forest, USGS Jarosa and
 Seven Springs 7.5-minute quadrangles

Access
● ● ● ● ● ● ● ● ● ● ● ● ● ● ● ● ●

From San Ysidro or Los Alamos, take NM 4 to the village
of La Cueva. Turn west onto NM 126, heading toward Fenton
Lake and Cuba. Nine miles from La Cueva, the paved road turns
to dirt; ten miles from La Cueva, the road turns north at Fenton
Lake. Continue on NM 126 as it passes the cabins at Seven Springs.
At an unmarked intersection three miles past Fenton Lake, turn
right onto FR 314. Follow this bumpy road through the Seven
Springs Hatchery to Seven Springs Campground, a mile past the
hatchery. Park at any of the pull-offs just beyond the campground
entrance.

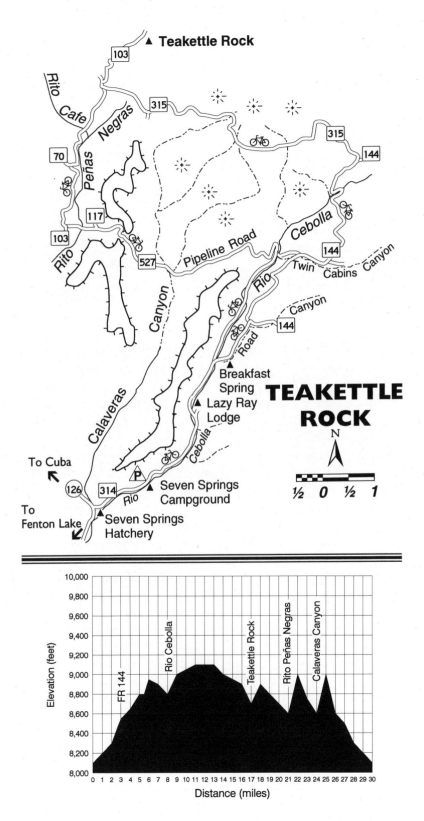

▲ Teakettle Rock

103

Rito Cafe

315

Peñas Negras

315

144

70

117

103

527

Pipeline Road

Cebolla

144

Rito

Twin Cabins Canyon

Canyon

144

Road

Calaveras Canyon

Rio

▲ Breakfast Spring

▲ Lazy Ray Lodge

Cebolla

TEAKETTLE ROCK

N

½ 0 ½ 1

To Cuba

126

314

Rio

P

▲ Seven Springs Campground

To Fenton Lake

▲ Seven Springs Hatchery

Elevation (feet)

10,000
9,800
9,600
9,400
9,200
9,000
8,800
8,600
8,400
8,200
8,000

FR 144

Rio Cebolla

Teakettle Rock

Rito Peñas Negras

Calaveras Canyon

0 1 2 3 4 5 6 7 8 9 10 11 12 13 14 15 16 17 18 19 20 21 22 23 24 25 26 27 28 29 30

Distance (miles)

177

Ride Description

▬ ▬ ▬ ▬ ▬ ▬ ▬ ▬ ▬ ▬ ▬ ▬

Continue by bicycle on FR 314. In one mile make the first wet crossing of the Rio Cebolla. Follow FR 314, past FR 380, then up the right bank of the river. At an intersection one-quarter mile from the crossing, bear left to recross the Cebolla. Now riding up the left bank, look across the river to a flat area above river level marked by tall spruce trees. This is the site of the Lazy Ray Lodge. More signs of the guest ranch appear in the next half-mile: a small earthen dam along the river, rock retaining walls, and mounds that mark the former locations of the stables and dance hall. Above, colorful tuff cliffs dominate the canyon.

A half-mile above the ranch, the road is blocked by a dirt berm. The old road straight ahead is the return route of this ride; bear right and immediately make another wet crossing of the Cebolla. Climb a small hill, crossing a trickle of water, then turn right on the double track heading up Road Canyon. A hundred yards up canyon, stop at a chimney where two springs cascade down the wooded slope on the right. The fireplace was used on Sunday morning trail rides coming up from the Lazy Ray Ranch.

Follow the double track through a fence and make the climb up Road Canyon to FR 144, which is reached 3.5 miles from the start of the ride. Turn left on FR 144 and quickly reach a divide above the Rio Cebolla. Bear right to parallel the deep canyon, passing open meadows of wildflowers. Another climb and descent leads to Twin Cabins Canyon and an intersection 5.5 miles from the start. Turn right on Pipeline Road, heading up canyon. Watch for tracks of deer, elk, and turkey in the soft powder of the road surface. In a half-mile, after a short, steep climb, take the left fork and continue on FR 144. Make a gradual climb, then ride a long descent, crossing a small drainage near the fence line of the Baca Grant. Climb and drop again, this time to the headwaters of the Rio Cebolla. Yet another climb leads to an unmarked but prominent intersection about 2.5 miles from Twin Cabins Canyon. Turn left here onto FR 315, dropping at first, then climbing to large meadows. After the road begins heading generally west, enjoy a view down one of the meadows to Redondo Peak to the south. The next five miles are gently undulating as the road contours the headwaters of many south-flowing creeks. Enjoy the forested route, and note the various types of logging practices, including a clearcut, along the way.

At a major T-intersection located about fifteen miles from the start, turn right on FR 103 toward FR 316. Ignore the prominent side road on the left and drop quickly. After 1.5 miles, just when the rider realizes he hasn't seen a rock in miles, Teakettle Rock appears on the right behind a corral-style fence.

After exploring the rock and its arches, backtrack 1.5 miles to FR 315. At the intersection, continue straight on FR 103, drop-

Teakettle Rock

ping through meadows, and crossing the Rito Cafe. Pass FR 70 on the right, then some private land on the left, riding 1.5 miles past the Rito Cafe to the junction with FR 527, the Pipeline Road. Turn left on FR 527, which soon drops to a crossing of the Rito Peñas Negras. Begin a steep climb over a ridge, passing FR 117 on the way. At the top of the hill, pause for a view of the Peñas Negras Valley and the ridges of the Sierra Nacimiento to the southwest. Follow Pipeline Road as it drops into Calaveras Canyon. A short way down the hill, the road surface deteriorates, and riding becomes more difficult. Tuff cliffs line the road on both sides, often wonderfully sculptured into strange shapes.

From the bottom of Calaveras Canyon, the road climbs a side canyon toward the next ridge. Riding here is made difficult by patches of tuff dust—weathered volcanic ash—which can be two or three inches deep. Pass FR 527F on the right, then begin a steep climb; the final assault on the ridge can be a killer. From the top of the ridge, begin the steep descent on switchbacks to the Rio

Cebolla. Use caution here: the road is steep and rocky with pockets of deep tuff dust that can cause a dangerous loss of traction.

At the bottom of the hill, turn right at the Forest Service shack and continue on the old road paralleling the right side of the river. (Pipeline Road crosses the Rio Cebolla and climbs the opposite slope.) Ride this enjoyable single/double track down canyon, making two more wet crossings of the Cebolla. In just over two miles, continue straight, passing the route up Road Canyon that was taken early in the ride. Backtrack the final two miles to return to the car park.

Background

Teakettle Rock is an isolated remnant of the Abo Formation left behind as the surrounding sandstones were completely eroded away. The four holes in the rock include a ten-foot arch and a natural tunnel that passes completely under the rock. Each of the holes began along the boundary between two layers within the sandstone, and were subsequently enlarged in the classic manner by weathering and mass wasting. The distinctive shape of Teakettle Rock created the legend that gave the rock its name. It is said that Pecos Bill used the rock to brew his green tea, which accounts for the green stains on the kettle's sides. The presence of copper in the rock is an alternative, though less fanciful, explanation.

The canyons of the west Jemez Mountains are carved through orange-tan Bandelier tuff, the same rock that forms prominent cliffs on the Pajarito Plateau on the other side of the Valle Grande. Tuff is a rock formed during violent volcanic eruptions, usually when a large volcano spews out so much material that its summit collapses. Massive quantities of volcanic ash, tiny bits of blown-apart lava, flow in glowing clouds down the flanks of the mountain. As the hot ash settles, particles may weld together to form tuff. Bandelier tuff was formed about one million years ago when the Jemez Volcano exploded, ejecting about fifty cubic miles of ash. Tuff is not very tough, and in fact is a soft rock that is easily eroded. Tuff dust frequently accumulates on roads and is more difficult to ride through than sand.

The quiet seclusion of the Rio Cebolla Canyon makes it difficult to imagine how busy the valley once was. A few miles above the Seven Springs Hatchery, a small grove of spruce trees on the northeast side of the stream marks the location of the main lodge and dining room of a dude ranch that operated from the mid-1920s until 1960. The ranch was built by a Chicago advertising man as a place to entertain his clients. Passing through several owners, the ranch remained small until it was purchased by Ray Craig in the 1940's. Changing the name to the Lazy Ray Ranch, Craig constructed a lodge, dance hall, and cabins to accommodate over a hundred visitors. The Lazy Ray was renowned for its rustic refinements, such as a fireplace in every room. Visitors fished for cutthroat and brown trout in the Rio Cebolla, cooled off in a large swimming pool, rode trails of the surrounding mesas on horseback, and, every night, kicked up their heels in the log-cabin dance hall. A special treat was a Sunday morning breakfast ride to a spring in Breakfast Canyon (now known as Road Canyon) for eggs and hot cakes cooked over an open fire. The Forest Service acquired the Lazy Ray in the 1960s. In 1972, the buildings were razed, leaving only crumbling foundations, the spruce grove, and the fireplace in Road Canyon as reminders of the canyon's more hectic years.

Further Reading

Pettitt, Roland A. *Exploring the Jemez Country.* 2d ed. Los Alamos, New Mexico: Los Alamos Historical Society, 1990.

Index

■■■■■■■■■■■■■■■■

Index

Index

Index

187

Index

Index

Index